THE
AMISH WEDDING
and Other Special Occasions of the Old Order Communities

by Stephen Scott

a People's Place book

Good Books

Intercourse, PA 17534

Photo Credits

Cover: front—Dick Brown; back—Richard Reinhold.
Richard Reinhold, 5, 17, 101, 117; Dick Brown, 31; Paul Jacobs, 39; David L. Hunsberger, 43; Grace Goulder Izant, 49; Fred Wilson, 53, 61, 114; Kenton Lavy, 67; Stephen Scott, 71 (all), 79 (both), 95; Sam Yoder, 83; Tom O'Reilly, 87; Craig N. Heisey, 102; Beth Oberholtzer, 109; Joanne Sinclair, 113; Harriet Scott, 128.
Map on page 123 by Stephen Scott.

Design by Craig N. Heisey.

The Amish Wedding
and Other Special Occasions of the Old Order Communities
© 1988 by Good Books, Intercourse, Pennsylvania 17534
International Standard Book Numbr: 0-934672-19-9
Library of Congress Number: 87-38310

Scott, Stephen.
    The Amish wedding and other special occasions of the Old Order communities / by Stephen Scott.
        p.   cm. —(A People's Place book; no. 8)
    Bibliography: p.
    Includes index.
    ISBN 0-934672-19-9 (pbk.): $4.50
    1. Old Order Mennonites. 2. Amish. 3. Plain People. 4. Public worship—Old Order Mennonites. 5. Public worship—Amish. 6. Public worship—Plain People. I. Title. II. Series.
BX8129.043S44 1988
264'.0973—dc19
                                                        87-38310
                                                        CIP

Table of Contents

1.
A Lancaster Amish Wedding

It was eight o'clock and pitch dark on a chilly October night. A gray-top carriage traveled north on Newport Road, its red flashers and red triangle warning motorists of a slow moving vehicle. But the horse pulling this vehicle was far from slow in comparison to other standardbred steeds. The driver, Levi Lapp, a young man of twenty-four, urged the horse on. He had already traveled eight miles from his home near Gap and the remaining four miles would take twenty minutes more.

Levi checked in his coat pocket to make sure he had the letter; without it his journey would be wasted. Just last week he had gone to the deacon of his church district to request this *Zeugniss* or testimonial letter, which could not be obtained until the fall communion after the October 11 fast day. Deacon Abe Stoltzfus took Levi's request to the bishop and two ministers in the church. Each put his signature on a letter, handwritten in old German script, which gave witness that Levi Lapp was a member in good standing in the Pequea Lower South District.

Levi was glad that the church had faith in him even though he had lived a wild life before his baptism the previous fall. Levi had run with the "Mule Skinners," one of the rougher Amish young people's groups, and had even played guitar in the group's band which performed at Saturday night hops. But now he was through with that way of life. Levi's brother Sylvan had always admonished him, more by his life than with words, that the life he was living was not right. Then after the terrible accident two years ago that left Levi's best buddy in a wheelchair and hospitalized Levi for a month, Levi saw the error of his ways. Against the taunts of his buddies he had joined Sylvan's group, the

4

"Quails." The Quail members did not feel that it was necessary to live undisciplined lives before settling down. Sylvan, although younger than Levi, had been baptized several years before him.

Levi had gotten rid of his guitar and fancy clothes. He no longer drove the car he and a number of his buddies had jointly owned. Levi started wearing a hat consistently and had his hair cut in the order of the church.

It was after he joined the Quails that Levi met Mary Beiler. He had observed Mary at the Sunday night singings, a tall thin girl of twenty-one with ash blonde hair and blue eyes. Mary wasn't the prettiest girl Levi had ever seen, but something about her attracted him. She was very quiet but not shy with the other girls; she seemed to be well liked. Mary never joined in the fun that some of the more wayward Quails indulged in (even the Quails had bad eggs). Perhaps Levi saw Mary as a source of the stability he so much desired. Levi wasn't sure if Mary would even consider a boy like him who had had such a bad reputation, but she accepted a date.

Amish church services are held every other Sunday. Every Saturday night preceding the "off Sunday" in Mary's church district, Levi went to Mary's house for a date. They often visited married brothers and sisters or cousins on their dates. In earlier times dating had been more secretive than it was now. Not long ago dating couples would hardly admit that they were courting. There was still, however, a certain reluctance to talk about the matter too much.

Sometimes Levi and Mary got together with their "buddy group" of close friends on Saturday nights. They did not, however, go to the hops or hoedowns that were discouraged by the church. Levi didn't often enjoy the privilege of taking Mary home after the Sunday evening singings. They lived too far apart to justify driving away half the night with a horse and buggy. But Levi's love and respect for Mary grew as they got to know each other better on their visits. She was far different

Joining the Church

Adult baptism is the way Amish and persons from other Old Order groups join the church. These groups, along with others that trace their roots to the 16th century Anabaptists, believe that baptism is the sign of a mature decision to follow Christ and to commit oneself to the church. Baptismal practices and beliefs of the Old Order groups are treated in more detail in Chapter 3.

from the girls he had dated among the Mule Skinners.

Levi turned onto Leola Road and passed two farms before he came to the lane of Isaac Zook, the deacon in the Mill Creek Middle West District. Levi really did not know this man at all. He had seen him only a few times. In a large Amish community like Lancaster it was impossible to know everyone in the eighty-four church districts. Levi nervously knocked on the door of the small western addition of the house, as Mary had told him to; Isaac's son and his family lived in the larger part of the house.

Isaac had been napping in a hickory rocker. "Ike, someone's at the door," his plump wife Katie announced as she pieced quilt patches at her treadle sewing machine.

Isaac laid aside the copy of the *Botschaft* newspaper he had been trying to read before he dozed off. He slowly stretched his short but wiry figure and shuffled to the door. He had spent a long day picking corn—a job which he concluded was almost too much for a man of sixty-seven years. Isaac's hair was thin and white, his face deeply etched. Not only had he seen many days of hard labor on the farm but his work as a deacon had involved a great deal of heavy responsibility.

The man opened the door and greeted the apprehensive young man standing there. The two stepped out into the yard. Levi introduced himself and stated the purpose of his visit. Isaac could have guessed; he anticipated such visits from young men soon after fall communion. Many had appeared at his door during his thirty-two years as deacon.

Levi explained that he wished to marry Mary Beiler and presented the Zeugniss. Yes, Isaac knew Mary, she lived only a mile and a half away. She had been their hired girl when Katie was sick last winter. In fact, Isaac's youngest son was married to Mary's oldest sister. Yes, deacon Isaac would take care of the matter. Before departing Levi looked Isaac in the eye and with a strained voice said, "Remember us in your prayers for the step we are about to take."

Early the next week Isaac walked to the Aaron and Barbara Beiler home. He would now act as the *Schteckliman* or go-between. It was eight-thirty in the evening when he arrived, and the youngest of the Beiler children were in bed. Mary and her oldest brother, Mose, were sitting in the kitchen with their parents. Isaac rapped on the door and Mose sprang to answer. He returned with a sly grin and told Mary someone wished to see her. Mose plopped in his chair and beamed over his magazine as Mary blushed and went to the door. Isaac extended his hand, which seemed a strange formality to Mary from someone she knew so well. Isaac seemed more businesslike than normal, although his tone was kind. He cleared his throat and asked if it was true that she and Levi Lapp planned to be married. Mary verified this report. Isaac cleared his throat again. "Can you say that you have remained pure?"

It was never easy for him to ask this. But Mary could look Isaac in the eye and honestly answer in the affirmative. This was all Isaac needed, and he was soon on his way. He sometimes had the unpleasant task of telling a young woman that she would need to change the way she dressed before the marriage could be performed, but this was not necessary in Mary's case.

Mary was glad she could answer yes to the deacon's second question. She could not imagine the shame of having to confess in church the sin of impurity and not being able to wear a white cape and apron nor have the evening part of the wedding.

Back in May, Mary had shyly told her mother about her plans to marry Levi. Aaron and Barbara Beiler had known about their daughter's relationship with Levi Lapp, but had made it a point to stay in the kitchen while Levi and Mary visited in the parlor on Saturday nights. The Beilers were concerned that Mary would marry a young man who would be a good husband and father and a loyal member of the church. They had some misgivings about Levi at first, but soon became convinced that he had truly had a change of heart. Levi's conversion was obvious to the whole community.

Preparations

The bride's parents play a very big part in an Amish wedding and do much planning and work long before the big day. One item of preparation must be taken care of up to half a year in advance—planting the celery. Lots and lots of celery is needed for an Amish wedding feast. Ordinarily a family will plant about one hundred stalks of celery in late June or early July, but for a wedding three hundred stalks are needed. When neighbors observe an abundance of celery in the garden it is the occasion for some good-natured teasing.

Another difficult task for the Beilers and Mary was choosing a date for the wedding. For Lancaster County Amish the options are very limited. The main wedding season is in November and December, although some weddings are held in late October and a few in January (rarely later). And then weddings are held only on Tuesdays and Thursdays. Mary and her parents needed to pick a date that did not conflict with the weddings of relatives, and it certainly wouldn't do if a niece or nephew were scheduled to be born on the wedding day! Finally the three decided on November 4.

The next decision was how many guests to invite. The Beiler home was large and roomy, and the porch could be sealed off with plywood and sheets of plastic for extra space. Yes, all the people in the church district sixteen years old and over could be invited and there would still be room for Mary's twenty-six young cousins. Special care had to be taken that there were an equal number of male and female youth, so they could be paired off at the table. Mary had gotten a list of Levi's relatives and friends to include. Relatives and friends living at a distance would be invited by a simple postcard.

Two weeks before the wedding, Levi and Mary took the bus to Lancaster to apply for their marriage license. They were delighted and amused to see more than a dozen other Amish couples waiting in line at the courthouse.

Although it had been months since Levi and Mary decided to get married, their plans were not made public until the week of their trip to town. On the second Sunday after fall communion, there was a very special event at the regular church service in each district. This was the "publishing" of couples who planned to be married. A breathless hush fell over the congregation at the conclusion of the service in Mary's district. After announcing the next place of meeting, deacon Isaac named the three couples who were to be married in the district that year, including Levi Lapp and Mary Beiler. Isaac ended the publishing by saying, "The couples have requested to be remembered in prayer, so we will want to do so for them."

When the deacon was finished Aaron Beiler invited all those in the church district age sixteen and over to the November 4 wedding. Joe Zook announced a November 14 wedding for his daughter but invited

The Wedding Season

Farm work, religious beliefs, logistics and tradition all play a role in limiting wedding dates for the Lancaster Amish. It is inconvenient to hold weddings before the last of the harvest work—corn picking—is completed. After Christmas, severe weather can make travel difficult. A full day is needed to prepare for a wedding, and making these arrangements on a Sunday would be considered sacreligious. That leaves out Monday. Many weddings are held on Tuesday; but Wednesday is out because people involved in a Tuesday wedding would be cleaning up from the previous day and those preparing for a Wednesday wedding could not attend on Tuesday. Thursday is a good day, but a wedding could not be held on Saturday because there could be no cleaning up on Sunday. As for Friday, weddings have simply never been held on that day.

Attendants and Helpers

All the attendants at an Amish wedding are of equal importance; there is no best man or maid of honor. Meals are not catered, so friends or family members must serve as cooks and waiters. There are many other jobs that are designated for certain people but may have to be shifted around if some of the people don't show up. There is no R.S.V.P. connected with an invitation to an Amish wedding, and some people may be invited to several weddings on the same day.

only church members over the age of eighteen since his house was smaller. John Stoltzfus then extended an invitation to his daughter's November 17 wedding.

Mary was not present to hear this. It was customary for the bride to remain home on the day she was published. Levi did not attend church in his district either, although the wedding was not announced there. Instead, he and Mary had dinner together at her home while the rest of the family was at church. Levi stayed until the Beilers came home. This would be his first official meeting with Mary's family. Between the publishing and the wedding, Levi and Mary could appear in public with each other, although they would not normally attend church services together. On the evening of the announcement they attended Sunday evening singing for the last time as singles, taking the opportunity to invite their closest friends to the wedding.

Planning now began in earnest. Many choices remained to be made. Two single young men and two single young women had to be chosen as attendants—called *Newehockers* or *Newesitzers* (side sitters) in Pennsylvania German. According to custom, these could not be dating couples. Mary chose her brother Mose and her cousin Rachel Stoltzfus, and Levi picked his sister Malinda and brother Sylvan. All the various helpers also had to be decided on, including the *Forgeher* or ushers, the waiters, the "roast" cooks, the potato cooks, the men who would set up the tables, the women who would take care of the tablecloths and the *Hostlers* (the boys who would take care of the horses.)

Back in September Mary had selected the material for her wedding dress at a local Amish dry goods store. She chose a navy blue fabric. Levi had ordered his wedding suit even earlier from an elderly widow.

As November 4 approached, the Beilers began readying the home place for the special day. Aaron and the other men enclosed the porch to provide more room. Barbara and the women gave the house a thorough cleaning, knowing that nearly every room would be used. Many parts of the house received a new coat of paint.

The day before the wedding arrived with the Beilers still feeling unprepared. Levi was on hand as he had been more often than not since the publishing. The bride's attendants and some of the table waiters were on the scene to help out, as were assorted uncles and aunts and some close neighbors. Friends brought the bench wagon from the home church district to the Beiler house, along with the bench wagon from a neighboring district to the south; more seating would be needed than for the usual Sunday church service. Men unloaded the benches, unfolding the legs before carefully arranging them in the house according to a precise plan. More than three hundred people would be squeezed into the house, and every inch counted. Much of the furniture was removed from the house and stored in the cleaner outbuildings on the farm. Smaller items were placed in the bench wagons.

Early in the morning Levi was given a traditional but unpleasant task that the groom must perform: cutting off the heads of the chickens. Since thirty-five chickens were needed, Levi became quite proficient at decapitating the fowl. A group of men gathered to make sure he severed the head with one chop. (Although few put much stock in it, the old

The Wedding Dress

The bride usually makes her own dress and buys identical material for her attendants. Navy blue, purple and other shades of blue are typical colors for the wedding dress, which is identical in style to the dresses worn for church. The bride and her attendants wear white capes and aprons. In church districts in which black caps are worn, the bride switches during the wedding day from a black cap to a white one. All of the bride's clothing is new. In Lancaster a bride must wear the same kind of high-topped shoes that wives of ministers do. No one in the bridal party carries flowers.

Lancaster grooms and their "side sitters" all wear black suits in the same style as those worn to church services. Coats and vests fasten with hooks and eyes. Shirts are white, and shoes and stockings are black. However, the groom and his attendants wear black bow ties, an item seldom worn for regular church services. According to custom, the ties are purchased by the groom. The groom also wears high-topped shoes and a hat with a three and a half inch brim. His clothes, like those of a bride, are all new.

belief was that it would be bad luck if he didn't.)

Many hands were needed to prepare the chickens and the mountains of other food. The four couples assigned as roast cooks divided up the dressed chickens and took them home to roast them. A woman especially adept at baking was asked to make most of the four hundred doughnuts. Mary's aunts on her mother's side made most of the cookies. One aunt made oatmeal cookies, another made peanut butter cookies, and still another made the molasses cookies. Levi and Mary and the bride's attendants washed the celery. They also washed windows and raked the yard.

The Wedding Day

Levi stayed at the Beiler home the night before the wedding. He and the whole family were up at four o'clock the next morning to tend to the usual chores of the farm: feeding the livestock, milking the cows and so on. In addition, there were many last minute preparations to make for the wedding festivities.

The helpers started arriving at six-thirty. By seven o'clock, Levi and Mary and their attendants had eaten breakfast and changed into their wedding clothes. The members of the bridal party took their places on a bench by the stairway in the kitchen. Levi sat between the male attendants, Sylvan and Mose. Mary sat between Malinda and Rachel. As the guests entered, they went down the line shaking hands. The women then went upstairs to deposit their shawls and bonnets, while the men

Organizing the Helpers

The bride's mother is responsible for orchestrating all the work before the wedding, but she appoints an organizer, usually a close relative, to be in charge on the wedding day. The organizer will carry a list of jobs that need to be done and people who are assigned to do them. Most of the workers are women from the bride's home church district. There is plenty of work to do: potatoes to peel, doughnuts to fill, fruit to put in serving dishes and cole slaw to make. Workers must also prepare the main dish for dinner, a mixture of shredded chicken and bread that the Amish call "roast." (Other people might call it "filling," "dressing" or "stuffing.") Food for the wedding is prepared in the basement or a detached "summer kitchen" or wash house, rather than in the main kitchen; this way, the kitchen can be used for seating.

Guests and Ushers

It is not unusual for a person to attend two or three weddings in the same day. Some guests come only for the morning part of the wedding, others for the noon or evening meal.

The *Forgeher* or ushers make sure each guest is seated in the proper place, according to age and relationship to the bride or groom. It is also their responsibility to see that the tables are filled with people during dinner and supper and to take care of any little emergencies. Four married couples share these tasks.

congregated around the barn.

Outside, the six Hostlers eagerly awaited the arrival of each carriage. Having this responsibility was the biggest honor a fourteen- or fifteen-year-old boy could have. After each carriage driver parked and unhitched his horse, one of the Hostlers took the animal and tied it in the barn. The carriage and harness were not numbered as at a funeral, and each driver would have to match up his own horse and carriage when he left. The Hostlers' biggest job would be to feed the horses around the noon hour. Because there was not enough room to tie all the horses on the lower level of the barn where they were fed, the horses from the upper level would have to trade places with the others when it was their turn to eat.

Gray-topped carriages lined up in the yard. A few young people arrived in black open buggies, often called courting buggies by out-siders; most young folks now used closed carriages but those from the very conservative young folks groups kept the old tradition. A few of the guests drove black carriages and did not dress quite like the Amish. The men were clean shaven and the women wore printed fabrics. These were Old Order Mennonites.

Along with buggies, several cars and vans arrived at the Beilers. The black cars with black bumpers were driven by another group of Old Order Mennonites, the Hornings. The vans were filled with Amish people but driven by "English" (non-Amish) people. These had been hired by Amish relatives living in distant communities.

A few minutes after eight o'clock, the male ushers came to the barn to begin rounding up groups of men for the ceremony. The women For-geher prepared to bring the female guests downstairs to the living room, where the service would be held. Seating followed a careful order. The ministers took their places first, followed by the parents of the bride and groom, the groom's grandparents and other relatives and friends. Men and women sat in separate sections, as at regular Amish church services. Many of the bride's relatives were busy helping with the food and would be seated in the kitchen where they could go in and out as necessary.

The entry of the young people was a separate and very special event. The unmarried brothers and sisters of the groom came in first. Next, the couples who had just been married or published entered together, then went to their respective sections. Cousins and friends concluded the procession of young people.

When the boys came in, all the men except the ministers took off their hats. This act was said to signify that the dwelling house had now become the house of worship, because the whole congregation was gathered together. The ministers kept their hats on until the first song, in accordance with an old custom.

When everyone was seated, Levi's brother-in-law Jonas Esh announced a hymn number from the *Ausbund*. On the third line of the song, all twelve ministers in attendance rose to their feet and made their way up the stairs to a room prepared for them on the second floor.

Levi and Mary followed the ministers from the kitchen to the *Abroth*

Wedding Music

There are no solos or instrumental music at an Amish wedding, but there is a great deal of group singing. Relatives of the groom act as *Forsinger* (song leaders) in the morning service. Lancaster Amish weddings always begin with the singing of *So will ichs aber heben an, Singen in Gottes Ehr,* page 378 in the Amish hymnal, the *Ausbund* (the Amish designate hymns by page number). Usually, the congregation will only sing the first three verses of the opening song. The second song is the Lob Lied, which takes fifteen minutes to sing. The bride and groom usually enter during this hymn; there is no special wedding march. The congregation then will typically sing the sixth verse of page 378 and as many additional verses of the song as are needed until the ministers come back from the council meeting.

Tunes sung at the afternoon and evening "singings" are more celebrative than those used in the morning service. These parts of the wedding give guests a chance to sing their favorite religious songs and some with secular tunes.

Opening and Sermon

The opening and sermon are central to an Amish wedding. Both emphasize the basic Amish beliefs about marriage: that it is a serious step involving not just the couple but the entire community; that it is a bond that may not be dissolved until one of the partners dies (the Amish forbid divorce and remarriage); and that one must not marry outside the church fellowship. The subject matter for the opening is determined by tradition and does not vary, though the comments themselves differ from wedding to wedding. The sermon also follows a traditional format and always uses texts from the Old Testament and the apocryphal book of Tobit.

or council room. Levi and Mary felt a bit nervous as they met with the ministers, but the kind expressions on the long bearded faces reassured them. Each minister had a few words of encouragement and advice for the couple. Then the bishop in charge asked solemnly if Levi and Mary had remained pure. Yes, they both answered.

The bride and groom were dismissed while the ministers remained for council among themselves. At this time they decided who would take the different parts of the wedding ceremony. Levi's grandfather, Bishop Samuel Fisher, was chosen to perform the marriage, not because he was related to the groom but because he was the oldest bishop present who had not performed a wedding in this district. Levi's uncle, Michael Lapp, was given the opening or *Anfang*. Deacon Isaac Zook of Mary's church district would read the scripture.

Levi and Mary were met at the bottom of the steps by their four attendants. Mary's brother Mose took Levi's sister Malinda by the hand and began the procession. Levi and Mary followed, and then Sylvan and Rachel. They made their way through the narrow aisles of the packed room single file, the young men leading the young women, with the congregation singing the third verse of the *Lob Lied* (the second song at most Amish church services). The young people came to six matching cane chairs reserved for them and sat down in unison, the three women facing the three men.

The congregation finished the Lob Lied, then sang the sixth and seventh verses of number 378. The ministers reentered the room during verse seven. Bishop Samuel Fisher, minister Michael Lapp and deacon Isaac Zook took their places on chairs at the head of the bridal party, with the bishop seated in the middle. The other nine ministers sat together among the congregation.

Michael Lapp, only in his thirties, stood tall and straight as he presented the opening. Michael told the biblical story from Creation to the Great Flood. God created Eve as a companion to Adam, he said. Michael warned wives not to yield to temptation as Eve did, and said that the responsibility of parenthood is shown through the examples of Cain and Abel. He spoke of the consequences of the "sons of God" taking the "daughters of men," and called attention to the fact that Noah and his sons had only one wife each.

When he finished, there was a period of silent prayer. All those present turned around and knelt facing the bench on which they had been sitting. When the prayer was over, the congregation stood but did not turn around. The deacon now read a passage of scripture from Matthew 19, verses 1 to 12: "Whosoever shall put away his wife, except it be for fornication, and shall marry another, commiteth adultery: and whoso marrieth her which is put away doth commit adultery . . . What God hath joined together let not man put asunder." The congregation sat down when the deacon finished reading.

Bishop Samuel Fisher slowly rose and began the main sermon. His shoulders were stooped, his voice barely audible. Samuel continued the survey of biblical references to marriage. Included were the stories of how Isaac married Rebecca and how Jacob married Rachel. As Samuel went on his voice grew louder and slipped into the traditional Amish sing-song delivery. Samuel wiped a few tears as he related the story of Ruth and Boas—a favorite text for weddings. The elderly bishop picked up a German New Testament and read I Corinthians chapter seven, verses 1–17 and 25–40, which explains the proper relationship between husband and wife. He also quoted Ephesians 5:22–33, which includes the passage, "Husbands love your wives, even as Christ also loved the church, and gave himself for it" and, "For this cause shall a man leave his father and mother, and shall be joined unto his wife, and they shall be one flesh."

Samuel now turned his attention to the book of Tobit, one of the apocryphal books of the Bible. He drew inspiration from the way God answered the prayers of Tobit and Sara, who had severe marital trials. Samuel emphasized Tobit's advice to his son Tobias: " . . . take a wife of the seed of thy fathers, and take not a strange women to wife, which is not of thy father's tribe."

When Samuel came to the part in which the angel suggested to Tobias that he marry Sara, the daughter of Raguel, he departed from his text. "We have here two people who have agreed to enter the state of matrimony, Levi Lapp and Mary Beiler," he said. "If any here has objection, he now has opportunity to make it manifest." He paused. "Obviously

no one has any objection, so if you are still minded the same you may now come forth in the Name of the Lord." Levi and Mary rose and walked forward, holding hands. They stood before the bishop.

"Can you confess, brother, that you accept this our sister as your wife, and that you will not leave her until death separates you?" Samuel asked Levi. "And do you believe that this is from the Lord and that you have come thus far by your faith and prayers?"

Levi answered without hesitation: "Yes."

Samuel then directed his words to Mary. "Can you confess, sister, that you accept this our brother as your husband, and that you will not leave him until death separates you? And do you believe that this is from the Lord and that you have come thus far by your faith and prayers?"

"Yes," Mary replied, softly but confidently.

Now the bishop again spoke to Levi. "Because you have confessed, brother, that you want to take this our sister for your wife, do you promise to be loyal to her and care for her if she may have adversity, affliction, sickness, weakness or faintheartedness—which are many infirmities that are among poor mankind—as is appropriate for a Christian, God-fearing husband?"

"Yes."

Bishop Samuel addressed the same question to Mary. "Yes," she answered.

Samuel again quoted from the book of Tobit: "And he takes the hand of the daughter and puts it in the hand of Tobias." Samuel took Mary's right hand and placed it in Levi's right hand, putting his own hands above and beneath their hands. He continued with a blessing, "The God of Abraham, the God of Isaac, and the God of Jacob be with you together and give His rich blessing upon you and be merciful to you. To this I wish you the blessings of God for a good beginning and a steadfast middle time, and may you hold out until a blessed end, this all in and through Jesus Christ. Amen."

At the name of Christ all three bowed their knees.

"Go forth in the name of the Lord. You are now man and wife."

Levi and Mary seemed to radiate a blissful glow as they returned to their chairs.

Bishop Samuel took his seat and asked one of the ordained men to give a word of testimony. Three more ministers were also invited to comment. Each spoke two or three minutes, expressing agreement with the sermon and wishing Levi and Mary God's blessings.

After they finished, Samuel asked Mary's father, Aaron Beiler, to speak. Aaron's voice was strained with emotion. He thanked all the guests and wedding helpers and expressed his wish that the rest of the day might be conducted in an orderly fashion. Levi's father was also asked to speak, but could only manage a brief, embarrassed sentence. Being a quiet man by nature he found it very hard to express himself.

Bishop Samuel stood again and made a few closing comments. Then he asked the congregation to kneel in prayer. The prayer beginning on page 55 of the *Christenpflicht* prayer book was read by the bishop, as it is at the close of most Amish church services (sometimes 114 is used if the time is short). The congregation rose from its knees and stood, still facing backward, for the benediction. The meeting closed with the singing of the hymn on page 712, which speaks of the wedding of the Lamb—Christ.

Setting Up for Dinner

Each man assigned to set up a table knows exactly where his table is to go. The benches that are used to make it are marked with chalk (T1 for table one, B1 for back seating bench one, F1 for front seating bench one and so on). Each tablecloth is similarly numbered and assigned to a particular table. Five benches are needed for each table: two to sit on and three to eat from.

Vom Eheftand

Wan zwey glaubigen perfohnen in der eftand tretten wollen, die im frieden und in der ordnung von der gemein ftehen, werden fie zum gebet vermahnt dieweil eß Chriftüs eine zufamen fügung Gottes nänt, fie werden im abraht genommen und die ehepflichten der eheleit erklähert, und vargeftält wie fie follen lieb und leid mit einander tragen , und auch gefragt ob fie frey fin von der hurerey.

Dan Wan Die Ehe Beftehtichet Wird, Werden Bei Uns Die Worten Gebraucht.

Kanft du bekännen Bruder, daß du diefe unfere mit Schwefter wit annehmen für dein Eheweib, und nicht von ihr laffen biß euch der tot fcheidet, und glaubft das es von dem Herren ift, und durch dein glauben und gebet fo weid gekommen bift.(Anwort,Ja.)

Kanft du bekännen Schwefter,daß du diefer unfer mitbruder wit annehmen für dein Eheman, und nicht von ihm laffen biß euch der tot fcheidet, und glaubft daß es vom Herren ift und durch dein glauben und gebet fo weid gekommen bift. (Anwort, Ja.)

---

*Amish wedding vows from the **Gemein Ordnungen** of Lancaster County, Pennsylvania. See page 17 for an English translation.*

Cooks and Waiters

The cooks at an Amish wedding are neighbors and people from the local church district. The afternoon waiters are typically aunts and uncles of the bride and teenage girls from her church. The noon meal is the only time young folks work the day of the wedding. There are eight waiters and eight waitresses for the living room table and two waiters and two waitresses for the kitchen table. Three young married couples are assigned to the corner where the bridal party sits. These are called the *Eck Leit* or corner people.

The cooks seldom see much of the morning service. The eight roast cooks (four married couples) rarely can attend the service before nine-thirty. The six potato cooks (three married couples) usually exit when the bishop comes to the part in his discourse in which Rebecca slides off her camel—a story told at nearly all Amish weddings. If the potatoes are started to cook at this time, they will be soft enough to mash by the end of the service. Since the cooks must be in and out during the service, they sit in the kitchen area of the house. Everyone tries to be present when the actual vows are made.

The church service was now officially over, and the more festive part of the wedding could begin.

The young people exited quickly, followed by the bridal party. The young men went outside and the young women upstairs to make way for the preparations for dinner.

The men asked to set up the tables went to work with utmost speed and efficiency. Each man was assigned to construct one table made up of three benches placed side by side and elevated by a special trestle. As each table was completed, a woman covered it with a white tablecloth.

Tables in the living room were placed end to end around the walls in a sort of "U" shape, and a long table was constructed in the kitchen. One corner of the living room table would be reserved for the bridal party. This honored place was called the *Eck* or corner. Levi had secretly bought Mary a new set of china which she would see for the first time at the Eck.

Next, the workers brought out large chests containing unbreakable dishes and eating utensils. These chests were especially for weddings and funerals; several men in the community had the responsibility of caring for the chests and renting them out for these occasions.

Traffic was heavy from the temporary kitchen in the basement to the eating areas. Some of the smaller items were passed up the stairs bucket brigade style. Food for all courses was placed on the table: first, the main dish, bread filling mixed with chicken ("roast" in Amish terminology); then mashed potatoes—ten gallons would be used in all—and gravy (ten quarts). There was also creamed celery—a traditional wedding dish—along with cole slaw (twenty quarts would be used in all), apple sauce (fifty quarts), thirty cherry pies, the four hundred doughnuts, fruit salad, tapioca pudding and, of course, the standard bread, butter, jelly and coffee. Jars of select celery were spaced at regular intervals on the tables, so that the leaves formed a flower-like arrangement. A special tablecloth from the bride's hope chest adorned the Eck, along with three decorated cakes for show that were contributed by some of Mary's friends.

The most elaborate cake was set in the middle of the corner. Most cakes are decorated by Amish women, but this one was obviously bought from a bakery; it had "Congratulations, Levi and Mary" written across the top. Pretty dishes filled with candy, nuts, mints and fancy fruits were placed at the Eck, as well as platters of lunch meat and crackers and dip.

In a surprisingly short time everything was ready for dinner. The bridal party made its entrance with the six young people walking in single file, holding hands, in the same order as they entered the church service. Levi and Mary sat across the corner from each other, with Mary on Levi's left, the same way they would sit in a buggy.

Single women sat on the same side of the table as the bridal party, with single young men on the other side. Levi's father and Mary's father sat at the head of the table in the kitchen. Along one side of this table were the mothers of the bride and groom, the groom's sisters under age sixteen and his grandmothers. Levi's grandfathers and his brothers under sixteen sat on the other side. Family members sixteen and over sat with the young people in the other room.

When the tables were full, all paused for silent grace. Then everyone began to eat. Levi and Mary found themselves surprisingly hungry despite their excitement. Waiters and waitresses scurried here and there supplying needs.

After all had eaten their fill, there was another silent prayer. The tables were vacated quickly to allow the helpers to get ready for the second shift of diners. The dishes from the kitchen tables were washed in the sink. A double washtub was wheeled into the main room and dishes were rapidly washed there. Some people had been specifically assigned this job, but the waiters and waitresses also helped. Food was replenished and in an amazingly short time all was ready for the second

Gifts for the Couple

Very few gifts are given at the wedding. The bride arranges those that are received on a table at her home. A small slip of paper is attached to each item, identifying the giver. As additional gifts are received during the visiting season, new things are added until the room looks like the housewares and hardware departments at a store. There are usually all kinds of kitchen items: dishes, cookware, pots and pans, Tupperware™ and every kind of kitchen tool imaginable. A number of people give canned food. Then there are tools for the groom: a shovel, digging iron, hammer, screwdrivers, wrenches and perhaps a wheelbarrow. There are also rakes, buckets, kerosene lamps and other household items.

seating. In accordance with tradition, the *Eck Leit* or corner waiters and waitresses now sat at the Eck.

After dinner, the young folks had a free period to mill around and visit. Mary and many of the girls went upstairs to talk and admire the wedding gifts from some of Mary's friends. Mary and her attendants changed from their black caps to white ones. Mary would never again wear a black cap. She kept on her white cape and apron, but this would be the last day she would wear them, at least in life. These items would be put aside to be worn in the coffin.

While Mary visited with her friends, Levi chatted with the boys in the barn. Some of them were playing darts and other simple games. Both Levi and Mary handed out candy bars as wedding treats. An old custom, which Levi decided not to observe, was for the groom to distribute cigars to the guests.

Meanwhile, those eating at the big table had finished and a third group of guests sat down. The table in the kitchen had already had three shifts. Some of the guests needed to go home immediately after dinner so they could milk their cows. When everyone had finished eating, the tables were reset with a variety of snacks: potato chips, raw celery, apples, cookies and pudding. The cakes that had been displayed were taken away and three different ones were set at the Eck.

It was now a little past three o'clock: time for the afternoon singing. The girls waited, giggling, in an upstairs room. The boys went upstairs and waited in another room. One by one they went to the room where the girls were, took one by the hand and went downstairs. Some of the younger, shyer boys needed a little urging. The boys who were going steady did not choose their girlfriends at this time. Dating couples would be paired off in the evening. One always had a different partner in the afternoon than in the evening.

All the young folks sat in pairs around the big table in the living room. The members of the bridal party returned to their places at the Eck. The Forgeher distributed *Ausbunds*, thick German hymn books which have only words, no musical notation.

The first song was the one on page 508, sung in the usual chant-like manner. Next came the fourth and fifth verses of page 378, which had been skipped at the wedding ceremony because they apply more to after a wedding. More of page 712 was sung (it has twenty-three verses). The last verse of the hymn beginning on page 554 completed the standard repertoire.

Now the singers began to make their own selections. All the songs were from the *Ausbund*, but the tempo of the tunes increased as the afternoon went on. Some songs were sung to the tunes of old gospel choruses. Women as well as men helped to lead the singing.

In accordance with an old custom, Levi and Mary did not participate; this was the day they were to be sung to. Instead, they were kept busy opening dishes of candy and platters of meat and cheese, which they passed around the big table. There were also all kinds of novelty food items for the bride and groom. These included a kerosene lamp with the chimney filled with candy, animals made of Rice Krispies™ and airplanes constructed of chewing gum sticks and candy. Some children made miniature buggies of marshmallows with lifesaver wheels hitched to animal cracker horses with toothpicks. From time to time, Levi and Mary answered knocks on the window from youngsters begging treats of candy. The couple gladly obliged.

At about five o'clock the bride and groom left the table, thus ending the singing. The snacks were cleared from the big table and it was reset. The evening table waiters ate at the kitchen table before they began serving the main table. These were relatives and special friends of Levi

The Evening Meal

Fare for the evening meal varies more than that for dinner. A typical menu might include stewed chicken over homemade wafers, fried sweet potatoes, macaroni and cheese, peas, cold cut ham and cheese, pumpkin and lemon sponge pies and the ever-present cookies. Close friends of the bride's parents serve as cooks. Two women are assigned to each of the main dishes. There are a dozen or so cooks in all.

and Mary—mostly cousins and couples that were married the year before. The older people were seated first at the big table for supper; those who had eaten last at noon were served first at supper.

The parents of the bride and groom sat at the place of honor. Mary's parents filled the places that Levi and Mary had occupied. Women were seated to Barbara Beiler's left and men to Aaron Beiler's right. On the opposite side of the table the arrangement was reversed: men to Barbara's right and women to Aaron's left.

While the older folks ate supper, the young people relaxed and socialized. But Mary had an important task to accomplish. She was to make a list of couples that would sit together for supper and the evening singing. As she mingled with the crowd she asked some of the young fellows whom they would like to sit with. Some of the young men who were very intent on sitting with a certain woman made their wishes known to Mary before she asked. This was one of the few times that couples who were going steady would be seen together in the presence of their parents.

At one point, Mary's task was interrupted when a group of girls motioned for her to step outside the door. When she did there were squeals of delight. One of the girls reached under the steps and produced a broom. Now, according to the old custom, Mary had officially entered the realm of the homemaker.

When the older people finished eating and the tables were reset, the bridal party again took their places at the Eck. The room was illuminated by brightly glowing mantle lamps hung from wires strung across the ceiling. Many people had brought lamps from home to help light the room. A new lamp was placed over the Eck. This was a special gift to the newlyweds from the Eck Leit.

Three new cakes were displayed at the corner. This time they would be cut and eaten, along with the six cakes that had appeared earlier. Once again the young folks went upstairs, and girls and boys assembled in separate rooms. The Eck Leit waiter to whom Mary had given her list positioned himself between the two rooms at the top of the stairs. As he read off the names of each couple, the boy and girl came out of their respective rooms and down the stairs, holding hands. A second member of the Eck Leit stood near the table and told the couples where to sit. The young couples who had just been married or planned to be married during the current marrying season sat on the bride's side of the Eck. Those couples who were going steady but had no immediate plans to get married sat on the groom's side. Around the inside corner of the Eck were special friends of the Newesitzers. Cousins, young folks from the home church and singles with no special partner also had their sections.

Many of the older folks took great interest in this event. Sylvan Lapp, they noted, arranged to have his girlfriend, Annie King, sit by him at the table, even though Rachel Stoltzfus was his attendant partner. But Rachel and the table partner chosen for Annie didn't seem to mind. Manipulating the seating in this way was a common custom.

During the supper hour Levi and Mary prepared treats of cake, fruit and candy for their special helpers (the ushers, potato and roast cooks and the bishop). Mary felt a deep sense of gratitude and unworthiness for all the work done for her and Levi. She knew that she could never really repay the helpers, but as a married woman she would try to help at weddings no matter what job she were given.

Ice cream was served as a special treat for the young people at supper. Each couple shared a dish. There was often some hesitation about who would take the last bite.

There was no prayer at the conclusion of supper, but hymnbooks were distributed just before the guests had finished eating. This time brown books were handed out rather than the black *Ausbunds*. These were copies of the *Unpartheyisches Gesangbuch*, the hymnal used at the Sunday evening singings.

The first song of the evening began on page 323. It had ten verses. One tune was used for the first three verses, then another song leader

Gifts from Parents

Many Amish parents set a limit of how much is spent on each daughter. This may be anywhere from $2,000 to $4,000 (in 1987 dollars). Some fathers adjust the amount for inflation if there are a number of years between the first and last daughter. Some poor families receive help from other relatives to give newlyweds a good start. Wealthier families supply all new items, while others are satisfied with used pieces.

switched to a different tune for the next several verses. Still another tune was used for the remainder of the song. Most of the twenty-six verses of page 324 were sung in the same way. For the rest of the evening, the singers made their own selections. The tunes used were all of the faster type, such as "What a Friend We Have in Jesus," "Amazing Grace," "Sweet Hour of Prayer," "Precious Memories," "Jesus Saviour, Pilot Me," "How Great Thou Art" and "Beulah Land," as well as several secular Christmas tunes. The German lyrics had no relationship to the English melodies, and some of the tunes had to be manipulated considerably to fit the meter of the verses.

One by one the guests began to leave. By ten thirty there were only a few dozen people left. Very late in the evening many of the leftovers were set on the kitchen table. This was called the *fress* table. (To "fress" means to eat gluttonously.)

At eleven forty-five the singing finally ended. The men went out to find their horses in the barn. There would be no party games tonight, as was the custom in some Amish circles. Mary's uncles and aunts stayed around to clean the tables, wash the dishes and put away leftovers.

The happy but exhausted bride and groom spent their first night of marriage at Mary's home. At four o'clock the next morning, they got up to begin the big cleanup. The first job for the newlyweds was washing the tablecloths, towels and other laundry. Pranksters often made this job more difficult by removing and hiding parts of the washing machine. Levi had avoided this possibility by hiding the entire machine in the old chicken house, but Mary found that the wash line had been removed, tied in knots and thrown in the top of a tree. Levi and Mary were thankful that there had been no trouble with pranksters during the wedding. The Hostlers had kept a careful watch for any unwanted intruders; some of the boys had even carried containers of black shoe polish to smear on the faces of such uninvited guests.

All the benches and tables were removed from the house and the regular furniture put back in. The dishes were packed away in the chests. The group had breakfast at nine o'clock and most things were back in order by noon. It would take some time until everything was exactly as it had been.

Setting Up Housekeeping

Levi and Mary stayed at the Beiler home on Wednesday night, then attended another wedding on Thursday. They would attend eleven more weddings before Christmas. At one of the weddings several young fellows grinningly threatened to throw Levi over the fence. Groups of single men used to pass Amish grooms over a fence into the

Visiting Relatives

Visits to family members are prearranged, and as many as twelve newlywed couples may visit at the same time. Typically, couples will go to the first place on Friday evening, stay overnight and have breakfast there the next morning. They go to a second place for the noon meal on Saturday and to a third place for Saturday supper. The night is spent at a fourth place where they also have Sunday breakfast. A fifth place is visited for Sunday dinner. The newlyweds may or may not go to a sixth place for Sunday supper before returning to the bride's home. Some visits are also made on weekday evenings. The overnight visits are made at the homes of especially close relatives or friends.

The young marrieds talk, play games, sew and knit. A favorite pastime for the women is making cross-stitch cushion tops for rocking chairs. The men often help with this needlework. Many host families devise riddles, arithmetic games or tests of dexterity to entertain the couples. The hosts also take the opportunity to give the newlyweds gifts.

hands of a group of married men on the other side, to symbolize the passage from bachelorhood to matrimony. This custom had gotten out of hand, however, and often resulted in a virtual tug of war with the groom. Torn clothes were common and even broken bones. The ministers now officially discouraged the practice, though it did occasionally take place.

Several weeks after the wedding Levi's family invited Mary's family, including married brothers and sisters, to their house for the day. This traditional gathering is called the *infair.*

Lancaster Amish newlyweds do not establish their own homes until the spring following their wedding. Until that time Levi spent much of the time at Mary's parents but went home to his parents frequently. There was no honeymoon in the usual sense, but Levi and Mary went out every Friday to visit relatives, often in the company of other newlyweds.

Part of the reason that the young couples do not set up their own homes immediately after marriage is so they can be free to do this visiting and not have the full responsibility of maintaining a home. They also have time to get their house or farm ready. Levi attended a number of public sales and bought farm equipment and animals. By the time the visiting season was over, Levi and Mary were ready to settle down with their own belongings in their own home.

Levi and Mary found a farm on the western fringe of the Amish settlement and moved onto it in April. Many family members came to help load the hired truck for the move. Now the couple would "set up housekeeping." Levi would begin growing a beard and would sit with the men in church. This new family would be expected to take the responsibility of having periodic church services in their home.

Mary brought to her married home her hope chest—a cedar chest and a bureau which she had received at age sixteen and had been filling with textile goods in preparation for marriage. Her mother had provided her with several quilts, some of which would be kept for "good" and never put to hard use. There were also sheets and pillow cases—a general rule was that there be enough for three beds—as well as towels, washcloths, tablecloths, cushion tops and braided rugs.

Levi also brought a kind of hope chest. A Lancaster Amish boy gets a slant-top desk as a birthday or Christmas gift. This too is filled with textile goods and kept unused in a guest room until the boy gets married.

Almost all the furniture needed for a household was given to Levi and Mary. Mary's parents gave most of this, including a gas refrigerator and stove, a kitchen table and a bedroom suite. Levi had given Mary a set of flatware on her birthday several months before the wedding. He had also given her a clock the Christmas before. This would sit on a special shelf in the kitchen.

Levi and Mary also brought to their new home several books important to their faith: a large German Bible (Luther translation), a German New Testament, a *Christenpflicht* prayerbook, a *Lust Gärtlein* devotional book, an *Ausbund,* an *Unpartheyisches Gesangbuch* for use at evening

The Bride's Dowry

Several items of furniture are traditionally included in a Lancaster Amish bride's dowry. These are: a hutch for the kitchen—which is called a "combine" since the piece descends from a combination dry sink and cupboard; a corner cupboard and sideboard for the parlor or special living room; and a drop-leaf table. When communion services are held in the home, this is used for the bread and wine. In addition, the bride and groom are often given straight chairs and a rocker. Dowries provided for Lancaster brides tend to be substantially larger than those for brides in other Amish communities.

singings and a copy of *Märtyrer Spiegel* (The Martyrs' Mirror), which contains the stories of the spiritual forebears who died for their faith.

Levi and Mary didn't like the fact that they would be all the way across the county from their families. Indeed, they would be five miles from the nearest Amish family. But Levi was convinced that a farm was the best place to raise a family, and farm land near the center of the Amish community was just not to be had. Levi felt certain that other Amish families would move into the area eventually. More than a hundred new Amish homes were being established every year in the county, and the new families would need some place to live.

2.
Other Wedding Practices

The events described in Chapter 1 are typical of the more than one hundred Amish weddings held every year in Lancaster County, Pennsylvania. Levi Lapp and Mary Beiler are composite characters. Their wedding is notable both for what it includes and what it leaves out. For example, the bouquet, veil, kiss and rings typical of most North American ceremonies are not part of an Amish wedding.

A few practices vary from one wedding to the next. It is traditional for a Lancaster groom to give the bride a set of china, for example, but this gift is not always given at the Eck as is Levi's gift to Mary. The menu for dinner and supper also may not be quite the same at every wedding.

Amish couples who marry must be in good standing in the church. Because of this, some couples who have not previously joined the church do so immediately before marriage. It is possible for a person to be baptized in September, take communion for the first time in October and be married in November. The church leaders, however, do not encourage that baptism be thought of solely as a prerequisite for marriage.

Weddings Outside of Lancaster

In other Amish communities the general wedding procedure is basically the same as Lancaster, but there are several significant differences. The function of the deacon as Schteckliman or go-between is an old custom observed by very few Amish. In most places the couple

planning to be married go to one of the ordained men in the young woman's church (not necessarily a deacon) and discuss their wedding plans. This man sees to it that they are published two weeks before the wedding. It is preferred that the couple not wait until the Saturday before the publishing. Among the Amish of Mifflin County, Pennsylvania, the Schteckliman custom is observed, but the church official goes to the parents of the bride to get their consent for the marriage. It has often been written that the Schteckliman actually proposes to the young woman, but this does not seem to be the practice in any Amish group currently. In Holmes County, Ohio, the Zeugniss letter is required, but in many Amish groups the young man is not required to obtain a letter if he lives in the same community as his fiancee.

In some Amish communities, many young couples attend church the day they are published. In Adams County, Indiana, and Arthur, Illinois, this is the usual custom. Among the so-called "Nebraska" Amish of Mifflin County, only the young man attends church. He leaves immediately after the publishing and goes to the home of his fiancee.

It used to be customary among Amish groups for the young man to go about in his horse and buggy and personally invite all the guests to his wedding. The Nebraska Amish have retained this practice. In the more progressive Amish groups, printed wedding invitations are sent.

Wedding Dates

In Mifflin County, the wedding season is observed much the same as in Lancaster. In other communities, a wedding may be held almost any time of the year, although spring and fall nuptials are most common. Summer weddings are avoided among the most conservative groups, because of the problems of food preservation without refrigerators.

Thursday is the preferred day for most Amish weddings, with Tuesday a second choice. In LaGrange County, Indiana, Wednesday is also an option. In Arthur, Illinois, weddings are held Tuesday through Friday. New Order Amish weddings in Holmes County, Ohio, are nearly always on Saturday. This is to accommodate people who have non-farm occupations.

Lancaster is virtually the only place in which the church service part of the wedding and the reception are held at the same place. In other communities, it is customary to have the marriage ceremony at a neighbor's place and the reception at the home of the bride. In warm weather, the church service might be in a barn or shed and the reception in the house at the bride's home farm. Amish who follow this practice claim that it doesn't take any longer to travel from the place of the church service to the place of the reception than it does to rearrange the same place for the dinner.

Role of Parents

In Lancaster County, the parents of the bride have special privileges. They do not have to work on the day of the wedding and are able to attend the whole church service. In other communities, the mother of the bride manages food preparation the whole day of the wedding. Among the Renno and Byler groups in Mifflin County, and in the New Wilmington, Pennsylvania, area, the parents of the bride and groom do not attend any of the wedding ceremony, but spend the whole morning preparing food. In most other places, the parents of the bride get away at least to witness the vows, as do the cooks and waiters. In many cases the fathers do not help with the food. Among the Nebraska Amish, the father of the groom leaves the church service right after the vows and goes to the bride's home, thus announcing that the guests will soon arrive.

In Kalona, Iowa, and Arthur, Illinois, members of the bridal party do not greet the guests as they come in. In Kalona they remain upstairs until their entry to the wedding. The identity of the attendants is supposed to be a surprise. It is also the unique custom in Kalona for the bridal party to sit in a single row facing the ministers. In Adams County, Indiana, the bridal party sits in assigned places in the main room before the bride and groom follow the ministers to the council room.

In reverse order from the way it is done in Lancaster, song 508 is sung first and 378 third in most Amish communities. The order in which other wedding songs are sung also varies somewhat from one community to the next.

Blue is the traditional color for Amish wedding dresses in most communities. The more conservative groups, prefer dark or navy blue. In LaGrange County, Indiana, and Kalona, Iowa, brown and gray are sometimes worn. In the Amish settlements established by nineteenth century immigrants from Europe, black wedding dresses are traditional. These settlements include the Adams, Allen and Daviess communities in Indiana and the Milverton settlement in Ontario. The Amish of Aylmer, Ontario, also follow this custom. A custom observed in most Amish communities except Lancaster is for the bridal party to stand while the rest of the congregation kneels for prayer, and for the party to sit when the other people stand for the Bible reading and benediction. In the "Swiss" communities (Adams, Allen, Daviess and several smaller communities) it is not customary for anyone to stand for the Bible reading or benediction.

Reception Practices

Because the wedding ceremony and reception are held at two different places in Amish settlements outside Lancaster, more time and space are available to set up tables. Usually, no more than two seatings are required for the noon meal, and sometimes everyone can eat at the first table.

The food served at Amish wedding dinners differs widely from community to community (see chart). Large amounts of celery are served only in Lancaster.

Decorations at the Eck also vary considerably. Fruit arrangements in fancy bowls and other items in decorative dishes are typical. Decorated wedding cakes are seen in most communities; however, the Troyer Amish have only plain cakes and the Nebraska Amish have no cakes. In Milverton, Ontario, it is customary for the bride to make her own wedding cake and one for each of her female attendants. Flowers and candles at the Eck are common in Holmes, Geauga and LaGrange counties, but some ministers discourage this practice. Wooden plaques with the names of the bride and groom and their attendants are often placed above the Eck in LaGrange.

At Milverton, very small stemmed glasses of wine are still served at the Eck. Wine also is occasionally served at weddings of the main group of Amish in Holmes County.

In Holmes and LaGrange counties and in Arthur, the largest groups of Amish often dispense with the evening supper. It is said that this is omitted in order to avoid the rowdiness which sometimes goes along with the later activities. The Swartzentruber and Troyer groups, by contrast, have an additional meal at midnight. This is the final activity of the wedding.

In most communities the same helpers work the whole wedding day, rather than switching off with other people as in Lancaster. It is said among the Amish that men help with the work much more in Lancaster than in other communities.

Like the Lancaster Amish, the Nebraska Amish do not ordinarily bring gifts to the wedding. Instead, gifts are given to the newlyweds when they make their visiting rounds. In other communities the bride and groom open their gifts in the afternoon, and people may see the items displayed in a bedroom.

In most Amish communities the newlyweds set up housekeeping very soon after the wedding. There is no visiting season.

Similarly, the customs of throwing the groom over a fence and having the bride step over a broomstick are unknown in most Amish settlements. However, both traditions are observed in Adams County, Indiana, and in Buchanan County, Iowa, the broomstick trick is occasionally practiced. In Holmes County, tricks are often played on the bride and groom as they sit at the table. These pranks may include

Typical Amish Wedding Menus

Community	Dinner	Supper
Nebraska Amish Mifflin Co., PA	Duck, chicken, turkey, mashed potatoes, gravy, filling, mixed pickles, cole slaw, apple sauce, peaches, prunes, cracker pudding, donuts, pie	Meat loaf, jello, fruit salad, cookies
Holmes Co., OH	Chicken, mashed potatoes, dressing, gravy, salad, vegetable, jello salad and/or pudding, cold sliced meat, cheese, carrots, celery, cake, fruit, pie, ice cream	Noodles, potato salad, meat loaf, cake, fruit, ice cream with strawberries
LaGrange Co., IN	Chicken or meat loaf, mashed potatoes, dressing, gravy, noodles, peas, corn or beans, cheese, celery, potato or macaroni salad, carrot salad, fruit and jello, cake, pie	Ham, potatoes, leftovers from dinner, ice cream with strawberries, cake, pie
Adams Co., IN	Meat (chicken, ham, smoked sausage or meat loaf), mashed potatoes, dressing, gravy, vegetable, noodles, jello salad, lettuce, cheese, celery, cookies, cake, pie, pudding, "knee patches" (fried dough discs)	The same as dinner but with a different meat
Buchanan Co., IA	Chicken or mock steak, mashed potatoes, dressing, gravy, noodles, vegetable, salad, applesauce, prunes, celery, fruit, pudding, cake, pie (bridal table gets breaded fish)	Leftovers from dinner, wieners, pork-n-beans, potato chips, ice cream

putting rubber spiders in the gravy or chewing gum in the salad. In addition, the newlywed's buggy is sometimes decorated in Holmes. In LaGrange County, it used to be the custom for young men to come to weddings and pound on saw blades until they got a treat. This was called "belling." Many Amish oppose such forms of frivolity and try to prevent them from being practiced.

Old Order Mennonite Weddings

During the last quarter of the nineteenth century, a number of groups withdrew from the largest group of Mennonites in North America (the Mennonite Church). These people wished to avoid the progressive influences that were sweeping the church at that time. Today these Old Older Mennonites resemble the Old Order Amish in many ways. They drive horse-drawn vehicles, use the German language in everyday conversation and in church, and wear distinctive plain clothing. Unlike the Amish, the Old Order Mennonites have church services in meetinghouses, the men are clean shaven, and members wear printed fabrics.

The Wenger Old Order Mennonites centered in Lancaster County have traditionally held weddings in the home of the bride, rather than in their meetinghouses. The wedding season used to be restricted to November and December, but currently weddings are held anytime during the year except summer. However, weddings are rarely held on days other than Tuesday or Thursday.

The bride and groom wait in an upstairs room with their attendants and closest friends as the guests arrive. The dating couples invited come to the couple's waiting room and give their gifts to the gift receivers. The gifts are unwrapped and displayed on the bed or other places in the room. Samples of the wedding dress and second-best dress (worn alternately with the wedding dress for several months after the wedding) are made available to girls who preserve them in scrapbooks. The boys then assemble in one room and the girls in one or two others.

A person selected as an announcer calls out the names of two young couples chosen to serve wine and cookies to the guests. The male servers get trays of small wine glasses (like stemless individual communion cups or shot glasses), and the women get trays of homemade cookies in the kitchen or wherever the food is prepared. One couple goes upstairs and serves the young people, and the other couple serves the married folks. This custom is said to follow the example of the biblical wedding at Cana in which Christ turned water into wine.

The announcer then calls the names of each of the dating couples, who come down in turn and take seats on folding chairs in the largest room downstairs. An usher seats the married couples in another room. After the young folks are seated, at about nine to nine-thirty, the ministers and the parents of the bride and groom go upstairs. Here they meet with the young couple and go over the procedure of the ceremony. The bishop formally asks the parents for their consent to proceed with the wedding. He also asks the couple if they have remained pure. The parents and ministers then go back downstairs and take their seats.

The first two hymns are "lined" by one of the ministers: two lines at a time are read before they are sung. The second verse of the second hymn calls the bride and groom to come forth and is a signal for them to come downstairs. The couple walk in and take their seats on wooden chairs next to their attendants, who have already been seated.

It is traditional for a Wenger Mennonite bride to wear a solid gray dress which includes a cape and apron. Her white covering has white ribbon ties; later in her married life these will be black. The groom wears a black standing-collar frock coat with buttons, a standing-collar vest and broadfall pants. This is the first time he has worn a suit like this. Like all unmarried men, the male attendants wear conventional sack coats with lapels. (Bow ties had formerly been worn but are now rare.) The female attendants wear dresses different from the bride's dress. These are often of printed material, and frequently do not match.

One or two ministers give sermons before the bishop begins his wedding discourse. Unlike a regular church service, the deacon does not read the scripture.

The bishop invites the bride and groom to come forward. Then he asks them several questions and pronounces a blessing on them in much the same way as the Amish do. Also like the Amish custom, bride and groom take their seats while the other ordained men give testimony to the sermon. The bishop makes a few concluding remarks and closes with an audible prayer while all kneel. The final song is *Gnad, fried, und reichen segen* (Grace, peace and rich blessings). While this is being sung, the bride and groom go upstairs. All the young people in attendance follow to congratulate the bride and groom.

Tables are quickly set up for dinner, and an announcer calls out the names of those who are to be seated. There may be as many as three shifts at the tables. The bride and groom sit at the end of a long table, rather than at a corner as at an Amish wedding.

After-Dinner Activities

After the meal, the rooms are rearranged for an afternoon of singing. The bishop announces and lines the first two hymns. The other hymns in the wedding section of the hymnal are then sung, followed by hymns that are used at baptismal instruction classes.

There is a break in which cookies and wine are again served (by the same servers, but they reverse who serves the youth and who serves the adults). After this snack, the German hymnals are traded for *The Church and Sunday School Hymnal,* an English-language book. The bishop announces the first hymn — "Jesus the Wedding Guest." The older people leave during the English singing that follows. On their way out, they congratulate the bride and groom, who are seated near a doorway. Often the singing ends when the newlyweds are showered with a quilt-full of balloons.

The bride's mother provides supper. Afterward, more young people arrive for the evening. There are a variety of games and activities that last until anywhere from nine to eleven o'clock. Then there is usually square dancing, with musical accompaniment provided by a boy or girl playing a harmonica.

The newlyweds set up housekeeping soon after the wedding.

The Woolwich Old Order Mennonites of Ontario have wedding customs similar to those of the Wenger Mennonites. The weddings are held in the home of the bride, and the reception is at the same place as the wedding. After a couple's publishing, they go out in a horse and buggy to personally invite guests to the wedding. Handwritten invitations include the names of everyone who is invited to the wedding and specify who will serve as officiating ministers, attendants, waitresses, Hostlers and so on.

On the wedding day, the bridal party and waitresses wait upstairs and do not come down until everyone is seated. Six to eight couples typically serve as attendants. These are usually the only young people that attend the wedding. Woolwich weddings do not include a council session before the ceremony, and wine and cookies are only served before the wedding. During the afternoon singing, the bride and groom serve fruit juice and candy bars to the guests. In addition, children distribute oranges and bags of popcorn and candy. They are given a few coins by the guests for this service. The afternoon and evening singings are completely in English. For grace at the dinner table a German hymn is sung. The prayer after the meal is silent.

A Woolwich Mennonite bride wears a navy blue dress, as do most of the women attending the wedding. Most grooms wear a frock coat that has lapels and a turn-over collar. A black necktie is worn with this coat. A few grooms wear a plain coat with a standing collar.

Changes in Customs

Among the Beachy Amish and conservative Mennonites groups, a

number of modifications have been made to traditional Old Order wedding customs. In these groups there is usually a formal engagement period. Printed engagement announcements are also common, although there are no rings. The wedding ceremony is much briefer than an Old Order service. In some churches, singing groups may provide special music at the wedding or reception. All of the service is in English.

White wedding dresses have become customary in many conservative Mennonite churches, but some Beachy Amish wish to avoid this trend. Weddings in these groups are usually held in church buildings. The reception may be in the church basement or a community building or school cafeteria. The newlyweds usually go on a honeymoon.

The Horning Mennonites originally observed wedding customs similar to those of the Wenger Mennonites, but a number of details have changed since the two groups divided in 1927. The Horning Mennonites still do not permit weddings in their church houses. About half of the Horning weddings are held in the homes of the brides; the others take place at a retirement home operated by the Horning (Weaverland Conference) Church, where there is a room suitable for large gatherings. All services in the Horning church are in English. The young people do not go upstairs before the wedding, nor are their names called off before they are seated. The bridal party does meet with the parents and ministers before the wedding.

After the wedding, the bridal party lines up either outside or in another room and shakes hands with all the guests. Wine and cookies are rarely served at a Horning wedding, and multi-tiered cakes are discouraged. There is often singing in the afternoon if the wedding is held at the bride's home, but the guests usually go home soon after dinner if the wedding is at the nursing home. There is no supper connected with a Horning wedding. The bride usually wears a blue dress. Other colors are permissible but not white. The groom usually wears a plain suit.

Plain Brethren Practices

Like the Old Order Mennonites, the Old German Baptist Brethren have church houses but do not allow weddings to be held in them. Lawn weddings at the bride's home are common. Public parks and community buildings are also used.

As many as three hundred to six hundred guests may attend an Old German Baptist wedding. The ceremony, however, is simple and brief, rarely lasting more than half an hour. The bride wears a white dress that is often more elaborate than her regular churchgoing dress. In most areas, a meal is not served at the reception. Marriage between members and non-members of the Old German Baptist Brethren is discouraged but not necessarily forbidden, and ministers will perform marriages in which neither the husband nor wife is a member.

In contrast to the Old German Baptists, the Old Order River Brethren have not traditionally used meetinghouses for regular services, but frequently use church buildings of other denominations for their weddings. This is a recent trend, however. Weddings traditionally were held at the home of the bride, and lawn weddings remain common. There is more individual variety in River Brethren weddings than in those of most Old Order groups. The bride and groom have a great deal of freedom to tailor their wedding ceremony to their own tastes, although some couples favor more traditional weddings.

3.
A Woolwich Mennonite Baptism

It was a warm Sunday in August in Waterloo County, Ontario. In the Weber home there was a flurry of activity as Joseph and Ruth and their twelve children got ready for church. Seventeen-year-old Esther Weber carefully combed her hair and placed a white net cap on her head. She tied the ribbon strings beneath her chin. Today these ribbons were black instead of the usual white. She would wear them at communion, on Good Friday and at funerals; after marriage she would wear them all the time. But today they had another, special significance; this was the day Esther would be baptized into the Woolwich Old Order Mennonite Church. She would vow to be true to God and the church until death.

Esther adjusted the cape on her dress and took a deep breath before going downstairs. There she was met by children running to and fro making last minute preparations. Esther hurriedly combed and braided little sister Anna's hair and helped Mother get the small children into their coats, hats and bonnets. Older brother Sam had hitched the horse to the family's open wagon and gotten his own buggy ready to go. Esther helped Mother arrange the small children in the open carriage before climbing into the buggy with Sam. The two vehicles turned right at the end of the lane, and the horses trotted down the gravel road to Floradale. The Weber family fell in behind the Isaac Martin family, and the Amsey Brubachers joined the procession from a side road. Soon a line of ten horse-drawn vehicles was clopping together through the Ontario morning. This row of buggies and wagons merged with more equine traffic as it turned onto a blacktop road and continued north to the destination, the North Woolwich meetinghouse.

Esther was almost oblivious to the countryside this morning. There

were few words between her and her brother as they rolled along. Instead, she reflected on the steps she had taken in preparation for today's event. She thought back to the Sunday in June when the minister had admonished the young people to consider their relationship with God and the church. That morning she had promised God that she would seek a closer walk with Him and request to be a part of the instruction class. Being a very shy girl, she did not have enough nerve to talk to one of the ministers after the church service. But one evening she walked to the home of minister Abram Martin to tell him of her intentions.

Esther had not made her request soon enough to have her name on the list the first time it was read at church. On the second Sunday the list was read, her name was mentioned in only two of the eleven local churches affiliated with the Woolwich group. Like the Amish, Woolwich congregations only met every two weeks. Because of this and because the ministers had no telephones, it was difficult to update the list of applicants. A complete list was not read until the Sunday of the first instruction meeting. This time Esther's name was among the fifty-seven young people who had made their requests known.

The first instruction meeting had been at the Elmira meetinghouse. All the applicants attended this meeting regardless of their home church. On six consecutive Sundays, instruction meetings were held at two-thirty in the afternoon. Each week the applicants gathered at a different meetinghouse.

Esther remembered how awkward it felt to sit on the front bench at these meetings. Ordinarily the old ladies sat in this section, which was to the minister's right. Esther's normal place was in the back of the meetinghouse in the section facing the ministers. She wasn't sure she liked all the attention she got up front.

The instruction meetings focused on the eighteen articles of faith from the Dortrecht Confession of 1632. Each session began like a regular church service. First, there was an opening hymn — selected from a series of fourteen entitled "Einladung an die Jugend" (Invitation to the Youth) in the hymnbook of the Woolwich Mennonites, *Die Gemeinschaftliche Lieder-Sammlung* (The Brotherhood Song Collection). Then the deacon read a chapter from the New Testament.

At the first meeting, chapter 11 of the Epistle to the Hebrews was read. This passage relates examples of faith found among God's people through the centuries. A minister preached on the scripture, after which all knelt for silent prayer.

A second minister read the first article of faith, which recognizes God as the creator of all things. The minister commented on the meaning of the article and read related scripture verses. When he finished, he asked the applicants if they understood and agreed with the content of the article. Each in turn responded with an affirmative "*Ja*," first the boys and then the girls. "Ja, ja, ja, ja," fifty-seven times like the ticking of a clock.

A third preacher read and commented on the second and third articles in the same way. He also asked the applicants to express their agreement. When all had answered, he asked God's blessings on the promises which had been made and invited the other ministers in attendance to give testimonies and further admonition. One by one each said a few words while remaining seated. Then everyone knelt for a prayer, this time a verbal one from the last minister who spoke. A closing song was sung from the youth invitation section of the hymnal, then the minister pronounced the benediction. The time and place of the next instruction meeting were announced before the people filed out. Three more articles would be covered at each of the meetings.

During the closing hymn at Esther's home church on the Sunday morning before the last instruction meeting, the ministers filed out and went to a small cloak room. Members who wished to express their concerns or criticisms about the baptismal applicants could go out and speak to the ministers. A few older men went out first. After they returned, a few elderly women went out to give counsel. The concerns expressed were of a general nature. Specific complaints about individuals were handled separately by the ministers. A few girls had to be admonished that their dress was not in order, and a young man was counseled about his cigarette smoking.

At the end of the sixth meeting, the dates and places of the baptisms were announced. North Woolwich was to have baptism on August 16. Esther was in a group of twelve to be baptized there.

As Esther caught a glimpse of the meetinghouse in the distance, she remembered her experiences the day before. She and eleven other young people had met there privately with the ministers. The last two songs in the youth section were sung. The articles of faith were reviewed, and the applicants were counseled on the duties and qualities that should accompany their commitment to God and the church. It had been a special, meaningful time.

Sam pulled into the churchyard and waited in the line of buggies. Scores of horse-drawn vehicles were gathered here. Many were open one-seaters like Sam's. Others were open wagons with two or more seats. A few had black tops. These were owned by older folks. Sam pulled alongside the porch and Esther quickly climbed off the buggy. She hurried inside through the girls' entrance at the northeast corner of the meetinghouse. Here she was greeted by her friends Susan Bauman and Lydia Martin, who were also in the instruction class. Esther hung

The 18 Articles of Faith

from the 1632 Mennonite Confession at Dortrecht

1. Concerning God and the Creation of All Things
" . . . There is one eternal, almighty, and incomprehensible God—Father, Son, and the Holy Ghost . . . the Creator of all things . . . "
2. The Fall of Man
" . . . [Through disobedience] 'sin entered into the world, and death by sin. . . . ' "
3. The Restoration of Man through the Promise of the Coming Christ
" . . . There were yet means with him for their reconciliation; namely, the immaculate Lamb, the Son of God. . . . "
4. The Advent of Christ into this World, and the Reason for His Coming
" . . . The previously promised Messiah . . . came into the world . . . for the comfort, redemption, and salvation of all. . . . "
5. The Law of Christ, which is the Holy Gospel or the New Testament
" . . . In which the whole counsel and will of his heavenly Father [regarding human salvation] are comprehended. . . . "
6. Repentance and Amendment of Life
" . . . [No] external ceremony, can, without faith, the new birth, and a change or renewal of life, help, or qualify us, that we may please God. . . . "
7. Holy Baptism
" . . . [Upon] confession of their faith, and renewal of life. . . . "
8. The Church of Christ
. . . Visible Church consisting of those who . . . have truly repented and rightly believed. . . . "
9. The Office of Teachers and Ministers—Male and Female—in the Church
" . . . Each one may serve the other from love, with the gift which he has received from the Lord. . . . "

her shawl and bonnet on a hook in the cloak room and waited for the others in the class to arrive. When all were present they went into the main room of the meetinghouse together.

Esther felt the congregation's eyes on her as she entered the packed room. She held her head down as she made her way to the front bench and took her place with the six other girls who were to be baptized. In addition to net caps with black ribbons tied beneath their chins, all the girls wore new black dresses with black capes and aprons. This "suit" would be reserved for communion and mourning. The usual black shoes and stockings completed their outfits.

Five young men sat opposite the young women. The boys looked very much like conservatively dressed youth from the early 1900s. Their hair was closely cropped and neatly combed. Their coats were dark blue with lapels, turn-over collars and pocket flaps, but were cut in the traditional frock style in the back. Before baptism boys wore regular

10. The Lord's Supper
" . . . We are earnestly exhorted also to love one another . . . even as Christ has done unto us . . . which is thus shown. . . . "
11. The Washing of the Saints' Feet
" . . . As a sign of true humiliation; but yet more particularly as a sign to remind us of . . . [the soul's purification in] Christ."
12. Matrimony
" . . . Paul . . . permitted [it], leaving it to each one's choice . . . provided that it was done 'in the Lord' . . . amongst the . . . spiritual kindred of Christ. . . . "
13. The Office of Civil Government
"Be subject and obedient to it in all things that do not militate against the law, will and commandments of God. . . . "
14. Defense by Force
" . . . The Lord Jesus has forbidden his disciples and followers all revenge and resistance. . . . We are . . . to pray for our enemies, comfort and feed them. . . . "
15. The Swearing of Oaths
" 'Swear not at all'. . . . We are to perform and fulfill . . . every promise and obligation . . . as if we had confirmed it with the most solemn oath. . . . "
16. Excommunication or Expulsion from the Church
" . . . For the amendment, and not for the destruction, of offenders. . . . "
17. The Shunning of those who are Expelled
" . . . That we may not become defiled . . . but that he may be . . . induced to amend his ways."
18. The Resurrection of the Dead and the Last Judgment
" . . . All men who shall have died . . . will . . . be 'raised up' and made alive; . . . The good shall be separated from the evil. . . . "

sack coats. Sometime after marriage they switched to standing-collar frock coats. Each of the baptismal candidates wore a white shirt and a black necktie. High laced shoes and suspenders were also required parts of the garb.

About ten minutes before the service began, the ministers entered the room from a side door and took their places behind the long pulpit. Like everything else about the meetinghouse, the pulpit was simple, without ornamentation. The building had no steeple or stained glass. The walls were plain and the woodwork and benches unfinished. To accommodate the large crowd today, extra benches had been placed in the aisles of the youth section, as well as beside the stoves and to the left of the pulpit.

The service began with a song. The minister in charge announced the number and read the first verse. One of the song leaders, who sat with the other men in the congregation, began the slow German melody. He sang the first syllable of each verse before the rest of the people joined in. A deacon read from the first chapter of the Gospel of John, in which John the Baptist recognizes the divinity of Jesus: "Behold the Lamb of God, which taketh away the sin of the world!"

During the silent prayer that followed, Esther earnestly asked for God's grace and strength for the step she was taking. When the congregation rose from its knees, the bishop stood to address the applicants. He then stepped from behind the pulpit and stood directly in front of it. The twelve young people filed out from their benches and arranged themselves in a semicircle around the bishop. Although girls and boys were on opposite sides, Melvin Bauman stood beside his sister Eva. By prearrangement, they had sat at the end of the rows so that they would be beside each other when they stood in front of the bishop.

The bishop now asked the applicants three questions. First, "Do you believe in God, who created the heaven and the earth, and in Jesus Christ the Son of God as your Saviour, and the Holy Spirit which flows from the Father and Son?"

The applicants responded in the German affirmative, "Ja, ja, ja, ja, ja, ja, ja, ja, ja, ja, ja, ja."

"Have you repented from sin, and are you willing to forsake your own will and the works of Satan?"

Again each applicant responded in turn.

"Do you promise through God's grace and guidance to follow the teachings of Christ until death?"

All twelve responded with a yes.

The bishop and the twelve applicants now knelt for prayer while the rest of the congregation stood. The bishop asked aloud for God's blessing on these young souls. When he concluded, he stood and the congregation took its seats. The twelve applicants remained kneeling.

A deacon came forward with a pail of water and a cup and stood at the right hand of the bishop. The two men approached the first young man in the line. The bishop placed his hands on the boy's head and said, "Upon the confession of your faith, repenting and grieving of your sin, you are baptized with water, in the name of the Father, Son and Holy Ghost." When he said the word "baptized" he cupped his hands and the deacon poured a small amount of water into them. The bishop released it onto the boy's head.

The bishop and deacon repeated the process for the other four boys. When the pair came to the first girl, they were joined by their wives. The deacon's wife removed the first girl's cap. She handed it to the bishop's wife, reaching behind the bishop's back with her left hand while she lifted the second girl's cap with her right hand. The bishop's wife replaced each girl's cap after the water had been poured. As

Esther's cap was placed back on her head, a trickle ran down her cheeks and mingled with tears.

When the last girl was baptized, the bishop returned to the first boy, who like the others was still kneeling. He grasped his right hand and said: "In the name of the congregation, I offer you my hand; arise to a new beginning. May the Lord transform you from your sinful condition into the righteousness of his kingdom. Be therefore welcome as a brother in the congregation."

The young man rose to his feet and the bishop greeted him with a "holy kiss," in accordance with the Woolwich group's literal interpretation of Paul's words in the book of Romans. The bishop went down the line and did likewise to each of the young men. His wife kissed each of the young women. When all twelve had been welcomed into the church, they returned to their seats.

The bishop stood behind the pulpit again and read the sixth chapter of Romans. He spoke about the spiritual meaning of baptism and the Christian's freedom from sin. "Reckon also yourselves to be dead unto sin, but alive unto God," he said, quoting Paul.

There was another time of prayer by the bishop as all knelt. The service closed with the customary song, benediction and announcements. Esther sighed deeply as she rose to leave with the other girls. Something seemed different that she could not explain, only feel. Like Mary of old she would ponder it in her heart, as she strived to remain true to the promises she had made.

Baptisms in Other Groups

The Wenger Old Order Mennonites of Pennsylvania are closely related to the Ontario Woolwich Mennonites. The Wenger group, which is primarily located in Lancaster County, is considerably larger than the Woolwich group.

The Wengers hold four sets of instruction classes simultaneously every year. Classes meet every other Sunday afternoon beginning in late July. There are six meetings, with the last session held on a Thursday or Friday. At each meeting the bishop covers three articles of faith. All the ordained men present say a few words of instruction, sometimes on very practical matters such as courtship practices and even bicycle etiquette. The morning of the baptism, the ministers have a private council meeting with the baptismal class in an anteroom.

Dress for the baptism service is similar to that in the Woolwich group. The girls wear black dresses but not black cap strings. Boys wear conventional coats with lapels. In the past Wenger boys had worn bow ties, but now these are seldom worn.

The Wengers use a glass pitcher for baptizing, rather than a bucket and cup. At the end of the baptismal service, the bishop reads a list of the responsibilities of members.

The baptismal service always precedes fall communion. The day after they are baptized, the new members take communion.

In Old Order Amish churches, instruction for baptismal applicants occurs during the regular ministers council sessions preceding the biweekly preaching service. At the first church service after the semiannual communion service, those youth who wish to join the instruction class follow the ministers as they adjourn from the congregation. In most cases the young people have talked to one of the ordained men previously.

Nine instruction sessions cover the eighteen articles of faith and the *Ordnung* or regulations of the church. The full requirements of the church are presented at the third instruction meeting. After this the applicants are expected to abide by the rules of the church, and the congregation is asked to observe if they are obedient.

In Lancaster, after the church service following the third instruction, a meeting for members is held in which the names of the baptismal applicants are read. In most communities the names are not formally announced. The applicants meet with the ministers on the Saturday before the baptism, at which time all the articles of faith are reviewed. The last instruction class is held on the morning of the baptism.

It is the usual Amish custom for a members meeting to be held two weeks before the baptism is to take place. At this time the congregation is asked if it is willing to accept the baptismal applicants as members. The procedure for baptism is very much like that described for the Old Order Mennonites. In Lancaster the bishop calls each applicant by name before baptizing that person. The New Order Amish in Ohio adopted this practice in the 1980s. In some New Order groups the girls' head coverings are not removed during the baptism.

Most Amish baptisms take place during the month of September, with a few in August. In the Midwest there are also many baptisms in March and some in February. In these communities a church district occasionally has two baptismal classes in the same year. In Lancaster each district has baptism only every other year.

The baptismal practices of plain Brethren groups are significantly different from those of the Amish and Mennonites. Both the German Baptist Brethren (Dunkers) and River Brethren baptize by trine immersion. This means immersing the person three times, face forward, in the name of each member of the Trinity. The name "Dunker" or "Dunkard" comes from this practice.

The German Baptist groups prefer that baptism take place in a flowing stream to symbolize the washing away of sin. The River Brethren do not make this association and often baptize in ponds.

The German Baptists also have a greater sense of urgency about baptism than do the River Brethren. The German Baptists believe that baptism is an essential part of the salvation process. Converts have often been baptized in the dead of winter, when breaking ice was necessary.

German Baptists do not dress in the regulation garb of the church until the day of their baptism. Among the River Brethren a person may wear plain clothing for an extended period of time (often years) before he or she requests baptism.

Neither group has a formal time of instruction for converts. The ministers interview baptismal applicants soon after they have made their request. The River Brethren have an "examination meeting" several weeks before baptism, in which the ministers report their findings and the members discuss whether each applicant should be accepted into the church. The German Baptists have a similar, but shorter, meeting on the morning of the baptism.

River Brethren candidates make their baptismal promises at the end of the church service, before going to the place of baptism. The German Baptists "qualify" baptismal candidates (either in the meetinghouse or by the waterside) by asking them if they will abide by the guidelines of Matthew 18 in regard to relationships between church members. In both groups the person administering the baptism places his hands on the head of the person who has been baptized and prays a blessing on the new member.

4.
Choosing a Minister: Holmes County Amish

It was a simple statement at the end of the church service. Bishop Eli Miller announced where the next service would be held, then paused. "We have discussed the need for a new minister in our church, and suggest that the congregation pray and thoughtfully consider this until our council meeting."

That was all. But at the noon meal many of the young married men had less of an appetite than usual. Several sat starry-eyed into the afternoon. Daniel Miller was one of these. He was thirty-five years old and the father of seven children. Like everyone else in the church, he had expected that there would be an ordination. One of the ministers, Jake Yoder, had moved to Indiana three months ago and the quota of ordained men would need to be met. If at all possible, each church district was to have a bishop, two ministers and a deacon.

Daniel knew he must serve if he were called to be a minister. He had promised he would do so when he was baptized at age eighteen. At that time such a possibility seemed very remote. But, now, even though he did not want to feel proud or think more highly of himself than he ought, he realized he was a prime candidate for the ministry. Daniel was a successful farmer with a reputation for honesty in his business dealings. He and his wife were in good standing with the church. Their seven children were lively but well behaved.

These were not matters Daniel would talk about with anyone. Indeed he felt less than humble for even thinking them. No one knew better than himself his many faults. Besides, even if he desperately wanted the position he would not flaunt his qualifications or campaign. That would

be the surest way not to be chosen. As every Amish person knew, those who most wanted to preach were the least qualified to do so. It was not up to individuals to decide if they were called of God. Rather, it was the responsibility of the whole church to seek God's will in the matter.

Daniel and Amanda were quiet as they drove home in their black surrey that afternoon. The younger children chattered as usual, but thirteen-year-old Clara was lost in thought. What would it be like to be a minister's daughter?

No meetings about the selection of a minister were held for the next two weeks. This period (called *Besinn Zeit* in German) was a time for members to consider the state of the church before the council meeting. At the meeting the congregation would decide whether it was ready to call one of its members as a leader. If the answer were yes, the selection and ordination would take place at the communion service two weeks after the council.

The next two weeks were busy ones for Daniel. Plowing, harrowing and planting kept an Ohio farmer busy in April. But still the thought of being a minister weighed heavily on his mind as he followed behind his horses, milked his cows and shoveled in his barn.

Council Meeting

The council meeting was held at the home of Lester Hershberger on the last Sunday of April. This gathering was much like a regular church service, only longer. Such meetings were held twice a year—before communion—and as special situations warranted. All members were required to attend the council if they wanted to take communion. Exceptions were made for illness or other emergencies.

The meeting opened in the usual way with a hymn, and the ministers of the district retired to another room to plan the service. The singing continued through the Lob Lied. Then, during the third hymn, the ministers returned.

Sam Miller (not a close relative of Daniel's) preached the Anfang or beginning sermon. This thirty-minute discourse included the stories of Creation, Adam and Eve, Cain and Abel and the destruction of the world in Noah's time.

The congregation knelt for a silent prayer, then rose and remained standing while deacon Mose Mullet read Matthew 18. This chapter described how Christian brothers and sisters should relate to each other and how discipline was maintained in the church. Preacher Titus Troyer gave the *Altväter Lehr*, a lengthy sermon on the Old Testament patriarchs. He began with Noah's curse and continued through

Abraham, Lot, Isaac, Esau, Jacob, Joseph and Moses, ending with Joshua. In each of these stories he traced the themes of brotherly relationships and the results of disobeying God. He finished the sermon by reading and commenting on I Corinthians 5, which speaks of discipline and the way of salvation.

The deacon and bishop responded to the sermons, then Titus Troyer read a prayer as the congregation knelt. This part of the service closed with the benediction and a hymn. There was now a break for lunch. The people ate as quickly as possible so that the meeting could be resumed.

As he took his seat after the meal, Daniel glanced at the faces around the room. He felt a love for each person present. For the first time, he noticed the absence of Amos and Susie Schlabach. They had not been at communion the last two times. Daniel had observed Amos plowing with a tractor several weeks before, and there were other visible indications that he was drifting away from the church. By skipping council he would avoid a confrontation, but the church would take action. If a member did not demonstrate his commitment to the group at council, he was not permitted to remain in the fellowship.

Bishop Eli began the afternoon service by briefly reviewing the messages of the morning. Next was a period of confession. Two of the members had come to the bishop and admitted that they had transgressed against the commandments of the Bible and the order of the church. They had already confessed their sins to God and now felt the need to do so before the church. A third member had not readily acknowledged his wrongdoing but was admonished by the ministers when he was caught. It was considered essential that members have a right relationship with God and the church before taking communion, lest they partake of the elements unworthily.

The bishop called the name of a young man. "It is my understanding that this brother has transgressed against the order of the church by using tobacco. If this is not true, I ask to be corrected." The young man held his head very low and said nothing. Bishop Eli then mentioned the names of a young man and a young woman. "It is my understanding that these members have been guilty of improper courtship practices. If this is not true, I ask to be corrected." Both reddened but said nothing.

Bishop Eli had a very burdened look on his face. He cleared his throat and wiped away a tear before proceeding. "We regret to say that Amos and Susie Schlabach have been disobedient to the church and after being counseled and worked with refuse to comply." Eli cleared his throat again. "We have decided that for their spiritual welfare they should be put under the ban, so that they will see the error of their ways and may repent and be restored to the church."

There were sobs from several of the members, especially from Susie's sister. Irene knew that her relationship with her sister would be greatly changed. She would not be able to eat with Susie or have a close social relationship with her until she confessed her wrongdoing.

Eli then told the young man and the young couple to leave the room. He reviewed both cases, then recommended that the young man make a confession of his wrong while seated. He recommended that the young couple make a kneeling confession, since theirs was the more serious offense. Eli asked the other ordained men to express themselves on the matter. All agreed that this was the proper discipline. Then each member was asked if he or she agreed. After everyone had voiced approval, Eli motioned for deacon Mose to bring the three young people back in.

The two young men made their way slowly to the front bench on the men's side. The young woman held her hand over her face and quickly took a place on the opposite side. The bishop asked the young man to confess his wrong. He hesitated, then asked in a monotone voice for forgiveness. Eli now asked the young man and woman to kneel before the church. Both wept as they confessed their sin. The three were invited to take their regular seats after the confessions.

The ordination of a minister was mentioned next. Eli asked the members to consider whether the church was ready to take this step. He invited any members who had hesitations to express them when he and Mose "took the voice of the church"—that is, asked for comments from each member.

Bishop Eli now began to recite from memory the *Ordnung* of the church. These were rules for daily living that the church had drawn up so that members would not stray into the evils of the world. After the rules for all members, Eli recited the regulations that applied specifically to men and then those that applied to the women. He asked the other ministers to help him if he forgot anything.

After all the issues had been discussed and the Ordnung presented, it was time to take the voice of the church. The deacon and one of the ministers left their places and began walking down the aisles. The deacon took the men's side, and the minister took the women's side. Eli and Mose pointed at each person in turn. At this time the individual called on made a statement concerning his or her peace with God and the church, agreement with the standard of the church and desire to commune. Some asked to be told of any inconsistencies in their lives. No hesitations about the ordination were expressed.

After the two ordained men made their rounds, bishop Eli asked if anyone had been missed. The two men reported that there had been an *enniger rote* (agreeable voice). This meant that the church was prepared to take communion and to go ahead with the selection of a minister. It was not always this way. If there were controversies or unresolved issues, the congregation would not have communion—or choose a leader—until these matters were cleared up.

The bishop announced that the communion service would be held two weeks from Saturday. Communion was sometimes held on Good Friday but more frequently on a Saturday or Sunday in the spring. There was also another communion service in the fall.

Communion

The next Sunday was observed as a fast day in preparation for communion. In the Amish tradition this was mostly symbolic; the members refrained from eating breakfast. In Daniel's Amish group there was Sunday School on this day, as there normally was every other week. In other Amish groups there was no church service on the "in-between" Sunday.

The following Saturday was the day of *Gros Gma* (literally "big church," which indicates the length of the communion service). Daniel and Amanda were very quiet during breakfast. The older children too seemed distracted, while the younger ones were more noisy and uncooperative than usual.

After the meal the children were shuttled off to Amanda's parents, who not only lived in another church district but were members of another Amish group. To have family members in different groups was not unusual in Holmes County, where there were nine varieties of Amish. Amanda's parents had agreed to care for the children for the day. Even though Amish children were conditioned to sit through three-hour church services, the even longer communion service was thought to be beyond their limits. Besides, the parents could focus their attention on the messages much better without the distraction of children. Some parents considered the day almost a vacation despite the rigorous schedule. Daniel and Amanda felt like newlyweds as they walked into the Aaron Beachy home.

The first hymn started at eight-thirty. The ministers got up and went to the Abroth room as usual.

The first person to speak after the ordained men returned was bishop Eli, who remained seated as he gave an outline of what was to be covered during the day. This ten-minute talk was the *Vorstellung*. Minister Mose Miller of the Maple Valley District presented the Anfang. All the ordained men from Maple Valley were here today. There were also many other ministers present, because an ordination was to be held.

Before the communion season there was a meeting of ministers to decide which bishop would conduct communion services in which districts. The other ordained men of the district would ordinarily go to the same service as their bishop. It was a custom that ordained men other than those of the home district conducted the communion service. Of course, the home ministers were also present and assisted.

Mose Miller's opening covered the book of Genesis from the Creation to the time the rainbow was given as a sign. This was followed by a silent prayer with the congregation kneeling.

The main sermon was delivered by Albert Weaver, the other minister in the Maple Grove district. Like the earlier sermon this followed the story of the Hebrew patriarchs. This time the speaker drew parallels with the New Testament and pointed out scriptures that foretold the coming of Christ. One of the ministers concluded the service by reading I Corinthians 10, which connects communion with the crossing of the Red Sea.

It was now eleven-thirty. Before going to the tables for lunch, the congregation stood while one of the ministers who had not taken part in the service led a prayer of thanks for the food. The people filed to the basement; the men sat at one table and the women at another.

When the members regathered for the afternoon, Jonas Schlabach, the bishop of the Maple Grove district, rose to give the *Leiden Christi* (suffering Christ) sermon. This detailed account of Christ's birth, life and death prepared the hearts and minds of the congregation for communion. Bishop Schlabach was a tall thin man with snow-white hair and a long silky beard. He stood very straight for a man of seventy-two years. Jonas preached from the entire book of Matthew, emphasizing the high points of each chapter. He ended with chapter 26, which tells of Jesus' crucifixion. Even though he had been preaching for two hours, he poured out his heart as he related the details of Christ's death.

While Jonas was preaching, two deacons brought in a loaf of bread wrapped in a white cloth and a small brown jug enclosed in a black bag. When bishop Jonas finished his discourse, he asked the congregation to stand while he offered a prayer. One of the deacons untied the bread and cut it into long sticks. The bishop took one of these sticks, broke off a piece and put it in his mouth. Then he broke off more pieces and gave one to each ordained man present. He proceeded to give a piece of bread to each person, first the men and then the women.

When the bread had been distributed, the bishop asked the congregation to stand again. A prayer from the *Christenpflicht* was read. The bishop then talked about the symbolism of the wine and offered a prayer. Albert Weaver, who had preached in the morning, distributed the wine. All drank from a common cup. The ministers were served first, followed by the older men, the younger men, the older women and then the younger women. When all had received the wine, they stood for another prayer from the *Christenpflicht*.

The congregation was seated while the bishop made the usual announcements about where the next church service would be held. There was a closing hymn, but this was not the end of the meeting. Far from it. While the people were singing the deacons brought in four buckets of water, galvanized foot tubs and towels for the ritual of feet washing. This was one of the practices that Jacob Amman, the founder of the Amish, borrowed from the Dutch Mennonites after he established a separate church.

While the congregation sang, the people went two by two to the tubs and took turns washing and drying each other's feet. This practice was a literal observance of Christ's command in John 13:13, which says, "Ye also ought to wash one another's feet." Men and women washed feet separately, in pairs. Following the command of another scripture, "Greet one another with a holy kiss," the feet-washing partners shook hands and gave each other a quick kiss on the lips. This was not thought of as vulgar or perverse but as a pure expression of Christian love.

After the people replaced their shoes and stockings, they walked past the deacon who was seated on a bench at a doorway. Each person put some money in a black bag lying beside the deacon. This was a collection for people in the church who had special needs, such as hospital bills.

Ordination

The people gathered on the lawn and quietly conversed until the next part of the service. Ordinarily the Gross Gma would be over, but now the ordination procedure began.

When the congregation assembled again the bishop began by reading I Timothy, chapter 3. This tells of the qualifications of a minister. As Daniel listened to the list — "vigilant, sober, of good behavior, given to hospitality, apt to teach" — he wondered if he could possibly be qualified.

When the bishop finished his talk, he and the other ordained men filed out and went to the kitchen. A deacon remained with the congregation. The men formed a line outside on one side of the house and the women on the other side. A minister waited at each of the kitchen doors; one for the men and one for the women. The door was opened slightly as each member whispered the name of the person he felt was the right choice for the position. Each time the minister received a name he closed the door, walked to the bishop who was seated at the table and whispered. The bishop wrote down each name. When another member mentioned the same person, a mark was put beside that name. The ordained men did not vote.

When all the members had given their *Stimmen* (voices or votes), the bishop looked over the list. Those who had two or more votes were qualified to take part in the further proceedings. The bishop kept in strict confidence the number of votes each candidate got. It didn't matter whether a man received two votes or twenty, he would have equal opportunity in the final selection.

Bishop Jonas found that there were ten men who had received two or more votes. He carefully selected ten *Ausbund* hymnbooks which had about the same amounts of wear. A slip of paper had been prepared with the words from Acts 1:24 written on it: "And they prayed and said, 'Thou, Lord which knowst the hearts of all men, show whether of these two thou hast chosen.' " The place where the "two" would have appeared had been left blank. The bishop wrote "ten" in the place to indicate the number of men in the lot. He placed the slip of paper in one of the books, then put identical rubber bands around each of the hymnals and rearranged them.

He asked if any of the ministers cared to rearrange the books. Two men stepped forward and took turns shuffling. Bishop Jonas stacked five of the books and lifted them from the table. He asked bishop Eli to take the other five.

The two bishops led the way back to the congregation. The books were placed upright on a small table in front of an empty bench. Bishop Jonas held the list before him and read the names of the people that had received the required number of votes. "Simon Hershberger, John Miller, Isaac Yoder, Henry Miller, Andrew Raber, Daniel Miller, John Yoder, Samuel Troyer, Paul Weaver, Jacob Mast."

Daniel felt a shiver go up his spine. He leaned forward and buried his face in his hands. The bishop asked the congregation to kneel in silent prayer.

Daniel and the other candidates in the "lot" prayed as they had never prayed before. Daniel prayed as Jesus did at Gethsemane: "If it be possible, let this cup pass from me: nevertheless, not as I will, but as thou wilt." He could hardly imagine himself with the responsibility of ministering to the church. He knew that he would have to handle many problems and sometimes shepherd unwilling sheep. He thought of the times he had been critical of the ministers and realized that he too would be subject to fault-finding from others. He could imagine that some would find him too strict and others accuse him of being too lenient. Could he take it?

The prayer ended and all took their seats. The bishop spoke again.

"Now the ten of you brethren may come and get a book at the table as you feel led."

No one moved for several moments. Daniel could not find the nerve to get up. Samuel Troyer suddenly rose and strode to the table. He picked a book and plunked down on the bench. Isaac Yoder followed, then Paul Weaver, moving slowly and deliberately. Jacob Mast, Henry Miller and Simon Hershberger took their turns in rapid succession. There was a long pause. Daniel found himself rising to his feet. He went to the table and noticed his hand shaking as it paused above the five remaining books. He chose the book at the far left and took his place on the bench.

Daniel held the book tightly, with sweaty hands. He sat with eyes closed, oblivious as the other four men took their books. He opened his eyes in time to see the bishop reach for Isaac Yoder's book. The bishop would go down the line and open the books of each person in the order that they had chosen. When he found the slip of paper he would go no further.

Bishop Jonas carefully removed the rubber bands and opened the book. The slip was not there. He gave the book back to Isaac. Isaac exhaled audibly, as if he were deflating into a limp balloon. Paul Weaver had been through the lot before. He showed no emotion when the paper did not appear in his book.

As the burden lifted from those whose books had been found empty, an extra weight was added to those whose hymnals had not yet been opened. When the books of Jacob Mast, Henry Miller and Simon Hershberger were found empty, Daniel became so nervous he was afraid he would shake the bench. The bishop's large gnarled hand reached for Daniel's book. Daniel squinted to see the bishop's finger slowly open the book. Something white appeared.

Daniel's eyes opened wide. He gasped. For a few seconds he was paralyzed; then he shook with sobs. Amanda broke down in tears. Her sister Katie seated beside her gave her a comforting hug.

The bishop waited until Daniel could compose himself. "If you can accept this service, you may rise to your feet. I give you my hand; stand up."

Daniel felt new strength within him. He stretched himself to his full height and looked directly into the bishop's eyes. The bishop put his hand on Daniel's shoulder.

"In the name of the Lord and the church is this ministry given you. You shall preach the Word of the Lord to the people, encourage and admonish them to the full extent of your ability. You shall be a servant for the church, you shall help to work with the ordinances of the Lord. You shall preach of the forefathers at the required times, and help to preach at funerals where it is fitting and you are asked to help. When anyone wishes to join church, you shall teach them the ordinances of God and the rules of the church until such time as they become members of the Church. Our Almighty God will strengthen you in this work with His good and Holy Spirit, for we ask it in the name of our Lord and Savior Jesus Christ. Amen."

The bishop gave Daniel the greeting of the holy kiss and smiled at him warmly and sympathetically. Each of the nine men in the lot greeted Daniel in similar fashion. Some were teary eyed, some very solemn. All gave words of encouragement and support. The ten men that had shared this experience would have a special relationship with one another for the rest of their lives.

The ordained men also greeted Daniel. Each of the ministers had been chosen by lot in a similar process. There was little need to talk. Communication seemed to flow directly from heart to heart, out of a pool of shared experience.

The greetings continued, with all the men present welcoming Daniel and the women greeting Amanda. One by one the people began drifting away to their buggies. Daniel and Amanda were among the last to leave. It had been a very long day. They were both exhausted, but sleep would not come soon that night.

Other Communion and Ordination Practices

The communion and ordination procedures described in the story are typical of the New Order Amish of Holmes County, Ohio. The New Orders divided from the main body of Amish in the late 1960s. They are stricter concerning courtship practices and the use of tobacco than are other Amish in Holmes County, and they are slightly more tolerant than the Old Order groups in matters of technology. In most respects, however, they are a sub-group of the Old Order rather than a different type of fellowship.

Differences between New Order and Old Order communion practices are relatively minor. The other Amish groups in Holmes County do not have a ministers meeting to plan the exchange of ministers between districts. This is left up to the ordained men to decide individually. Nor do the other Holmes County Amish have a break for lunch during the council and communion services. The usual custom is for a few people at a time to go out and eat while the preaching continues.

In other groups and communities the precise order of service may vary, along with the specific hymns, prayers and scriptures used. But the basic communion procedure is the same among all Amish.

Likewise, there are minor variations in the selection of ministers. All Amish churches use the lot, but the number of votes required to qualify a candidate for the final selection may be either two or three. In the Swiss Amish communities in Allen and Adams counties in Indiana, only the two members who receive the most votes are placed in the lot.

The slip of paper that is placed in the hymnbook does not always have the same thing written on it. In Lancaster County, Proverbs 16:33 is used: "The lot is cast into the lap; but the whole disposing thereof is of the Lord." Also, it is the custom in many Amish communities to tie the hymnbooks with strings rather than to secure them with rubber bands.

The bishop of an Amish church district is selected from among the ministers of that district, except in areas such as Lancaster where a bishop is responsible for two districts. (In such cases, he comes from one of his two districts.)

A deacon is ordained in the same way a minister is. In some communities, such as Lancaster, Mifflin and Adams counties, a deacon is not eligible to be in the lot for the position of minister. In these areas the vows one makes as a deacon are not to be altered by accepting another position in the church.

The Old Order Mennonites select their ministers by lot, but do not combine the communion service with the ordination. At the council meeting the church decides whether it is ready to select a minister or other church official.

Votes are taken two weeks later. Unlike the Amish, not all the members are expected to take part. Generally only the older members go to the ordained men assembled in an anteroom and state their choice.

The names of the candidates are announced at the end of the service. The next day the candidates (called "the class") and their wives meet with the ordained men for an examination meeting. The candidates are given advice and are told of the regulations governing ordained leaders. At this time, anyone in the class may decline to be included in the lot, but this rarely happens.

The ordination service is held the following day. The Old Order Mennonites place the lot in a hymnbook as the Amish do, and the procedure for sorting and selecting the books is much the same. In Pennsylvania the books are placed on a table; in Ontario they are lined up on the pulpit. As in the Amish church, the ordination charge is given immediately after the selection is made.

Most Old Order Mennonite churches have one minister and one deacon. In the larger settlements, a bishop oversees several congregations. Since church is not held in every meetinghouse every Sunday, ordained men visit other churches on their "off" Sunday.

Communion services of Old Order Mennonites follow the same pattern as those of the Amish. Two weeks before communion, there is a council meeting at which members express their concerns. In Pennsylvania there is also a preparatory service on the Saturday before communion. At this meeting Isaiah 58 is read and the church rules are presented.

At the communion service the story of Christ's suffering is read (Matthew 26 and 27 or Luke 22 and 23), and one or more of the ordained men preaches about the Old Testament patriarchs. Then the bishop, assisted by the deacon, distributes the bread and wine (in that order) to each communicant.

The Old Order River Brethren normally have a bishop, two ministers and a deacon in each church district. In some cases it has been the practice to have two deacons.

River Brethren do not choose their ministers by lot. Instead, an announcement is made at the annual council meeting when the need for a new minister arises. Before the selection, a Sunday morning service is dedicated to outlining the qualifications of a minister. A week or more later, each member comes to church with the name of a person written on a piece of paper. Under the supervision of a bishop, these slips are placed in a box at the the entrance of the meeting place. Two or more of the ordained men count the votes during the beginning of the church service.

The person with the most votes receives the calling of the church. The choice may or may not be announced at the end of the church service. The person thus selected is not ordained right away, but goes through a trial period in which he takes the full responsibility of his office. The ordination takes place six months to a year after the selection.

The Old German Baptist Brethren also select their ministers by vote. When a local congregation feels it needs a new minister, the selection is made during a regular council meeting. Each member of the congregation goes to a small room in the meetinghouse and voices his or her choice to a group of ministers who are assembled there. Ministers from a neighboring church generally have charge of this procedure. An announcement is made to the congregation as soon as the votes have been counted. The member selected is then given the charge.

The Old German Baptists have three degrees of ministry. A person is elected to the first degree and may advance to the second degree upon the consensus of the group. In the same way a person is advanced from the second degree to the eldership. With each advance there is more responsibility.

The first and second degrees are a sort of trial period. A first degree minister may be given permission to preach and a second degree minister may also perform baptisms and marriages. Only the elder is fully ordained. The elder who has been ordained the longest is known as the elder in charge and has more authority than the others.

In each congregation there are usually several elders, one or two first or second degree ministers and several deacons. In one of the largest churches — the congregation at Covington, Ohio, which had 309 members in 1987 — there were six elders, one first degree minister and nine deacons.

A deacon is selected like a first degree minister. A deacon may also be elected as a minister, which often happens. Deacons take care of the financial matters of the church, caring for the needy and settling disciplinary problems.

Among the Old German Baptists and River Brethren, deacons are responsible for conducting the "annual visit" in the congregation. Each home is contacted by these "visiting brethren," who determine if each member is at peace with the church and willing to work with it. The members at this time may express their concerns about the church.

The communion practices of the Brethren are described in Chapters 5 and 6.

5.
An Old German Baptist Brethren Annual Meeting

The Jamison family arrived at the Bowman farm a little after seven on Thursday morning—just in time to see the canvas of the dining tent climb into the sky as it was raised to its full height. Mark Jamison, the father, pointed to two tall, rope-supported poles standing in the field, and assured his disappointed younger children that they would get to see the entire tent-raising process when the big council tent was put up. This was where the worship services would be held.

Eight-year-old John and twelve-year-old Kevin spotted a small skid loader at work near one of the tall poles. The tractor-like machine had a hammering device on its scoop that the driver was using to drive long wooden stakes around the perimeter of the tent area. The clink, clink, clink rang through the grounds, attracting an audience of children as the machine went from one stake to the next.

Seventeen-year-old Linda and her fifteen-year-old brother, Craig, saw groups of young people and wandered toward them. Mark and his wife, Betty, joined the several hundred adults scattered over the grounds, nearly all of whom were dressed in the distinctive garb of the Old German Baptist Brethren.

This was the beginning of the group's annual meeting, a time of worship, fellowship and church business. The Jamisons had driven ten hours by car from their Virginia home to this western Ohio farm for the gathering. Mark, a minister, was one of two men chosen to represent his church district as a delegate.

Last year's annual meeting had been held in the Jamisons' home community, but that would not happen again for more than a decade. The location of the gathering was rotated among four annual meeting districts: Ohio, Indiana, Eastern and Western. Group members were less numerous in the East than in the other districts, so the meeting was only held there every six or seven years, with Virginia taking turns with Pennsylvania.

Still, it was worth a long drive to attend the meeting, Mark thought, as he went to the dining tent to assist in the building of dozens of wooden tables and benches. Out-of-state people were not really expected to help, but Mark was a carpenter by trade and found it hard not to be involved. This was the tenth annual meeting he had attended in the last twelve years, but both the event and the preparations for it never failed to impress him. Here in the dining tent, thousands of people would be served free meals in the next few days. The tent had electricity, a kitchen for preparing enormous amounts of food, hot and cold running water and even a row of washing machines and dryers. Nearby, a temporary building had been constructed to distribute food and supplies. At a distance from the tents were two long buildings containing the restrooms.

Mark busied himself with a hammer and saw. Out in the field, John and Kevin watched as a huge forklift deposited a gigantic bundle of canvas near one of the tall poles. Other bundles were brought to the tent area. Dozens of men and boys began unrolling, pulling and stretching the canvas until it covered the whole tent area. Several men laced the different sections together. When all was in place several others slipped into the holes around each post. They tugged on ropes and lifted the expanses of tan canvas skyward.

More people went to work tying ropes and positioning additional poles inside the council tent. Hundreds of stakes were driven in pairs throughout the tent. Boards were placed on top of these stakes to form backless benches. The air was filled with sounds of pounding and sawing. Some men worked in twos or threes, hitting stakes alternately in rapid succession.

By noon the dining tent was sufficiently completed to serve the workers and watchers. The meeting grounds were nearly ready by this time, and most of the people went home after they ate.

Mark went to the "baggage room" which was set up in a garage. Here he bought a large map showing where the Old German Baptist families in the area lived. The Jamisons had spent the previous night with friends north of Greenville whom Mark had contacted many weeks in advance. This morning Mark had received several additional invitations for meals and overnight lodging, and he wanted to make sure he could find the places.

For people who had not made previous arrangements, there was an efficient system for finding accommodations. Behind a counter on a piece of plywood were dozens of nails with stacks of tags hanging on them. Each color designated a different night. Several people from the host districts stood behind the counter to help visitors find the appropriate number of tags. Each tag had a name, address, phone number and directions to the host's home.

Satisfied that he knew where he was going, Mark went off to look for several old friends that he had heard were on the grounds. As a member of the host district last year, he had been involved not only in the Thursday tent-raisings but in the last-minute preparations on Friday. Between this and the usual church services and business sessions, he had had little chance for visiting. This year he was free until the opening session, and he intended to make the most of his time.

Saturday morning found the Jamisons on their way to the official opening of the annual meeting. The usually quiet back roads of Darke County near the Indiana line were filled with cars driven by black-hatted men and white-capped women. At the crossroads in front of the meeting grounds, a young man directed traffic with a cane. Cars moved through a large grass field filled with hundreds of vehicles. Sections were marked off with numbers on the ends of poles. The Jamisons parked in section seven and followed the flow of people to the tents.

By nine-thirty the large meeting tent was nearly full. There was space for 2,500 people on the backless benches in the tent. Several hundred other people stood around the perimeter of the tent for the service. Some families sat together; others, like the Jamisons, split up with the men and boys on one side and women and girls on the other. In the middle of the tent was a long table surrounded by bearded elders of the Old German Baptist Brethren Church, who were talking quietly among themselves. The speakers for the opening service were not chosen ahead of time. Instead, the ministers waited for one of their number to "take the liberty" to speak. Others, in turn, would follow. Though there was no precise order, it was expected that the older, more experienced elders and those who had come from far away would speak first.

One of the elders announced the number of a hymn and read the first verse. A song leader who remained seated started the hymn and three thousand people joined in. After every verse the singing stopped, and the minister read the next verse before the group sang it. This custom, called "lining," was a carryover from the days when not everyone had a hymnbook or could read. The Old German Baptists believed that the practice helped to emphasize the meaning of the words.

At the conclusion of the hymn, a minister from Virginia stood and read a chapter from the book of Isaiah. He would preach the main sermon. A minister from California lined a hymn and gave a short devotional. Then he led the congregation in prayer. Some of the people knelt; others merely leaned forward, because there was so little room.

A third minister read a chapter from the New Testament book of I Peter. This was followed by the main sermon, which lasted about forty minutes. Two other ministers gave short responses. The one who spoke last lined a hymn and led the closing prayer.

Even before the concluding song, some of those standing around the outside of the tent moved toward the dining tent. Many had been standing there for some time. Since only about eight hundred could be seated in the tent at one time, those who wanted to eat at the first seating had to hurry.

Many people, like the Jamison boys, decided not to wait and bought food at one of the concession tents. These were run by people from a local Church of the Brethren congregation—part of the group from which the Old German Baptists divided in 1881. Unlike most of the adults at the meeting, the Church of the Brethren members wore no distinctive attire.

A special section in the dining tent was reserved for ministers. Mark found a place there, while Betty sat in the section for ministers' wives. The dining tent foreman for the day, a young minister with a very long beard, saw that all the places in the tent were filled. He raised his voice to be heard above the crowd: "One of the brethren will line a hymn and ask the blessing on the food." There was some deliberation at the ministers' table. Then an older man stood, chose a hymn and prayed.

Sounding rather like a drill sergeant, the young man in charge called out orders to the waiters and waitresses. Meals at annual meeting were always the same. The main dish was soup made from crumbled bread soaked in beef broth. On top of the bowls of soup were plates of beef chunks. There was also plenty of bread (white and brown), butter, apple butter and pickles. Dessert was canned peaches. Each place setting consisted of a cup, deep saucer, knife, fork and large spoon. The plain white porcelain dishes had markings on the bottom to indicate which local congregations owned them. These were ordinarily used at the "love feasts" (special services that included a communion observance) of the individual churches.

The waiters and waitresses were constantly circulating up and down the aisles distributing tea and coffee, refilling cups with water and replenishing food. There was a great deal of visiting, but most people tried to eat as quickly as possible so that the next shift would not have to wait so long. When the dining tent foreman saw that most people had finished eating, he called out for one of the ministers to line a hymn and

71

return thanks. The people exited, and the dishes were washed in dish-pans at each table. A row of water spigots, each with its own water heater, was located between the men's and women's sections in the center of the tent. The tables were rapidly reset, and the second group entered.

After lunch, there was time to renew acquaintances and make new friends. Many people continued to visit outside after the next meeting was called to order at two o'clock. Even with an additional worship service held simultaneously in a large implement building, there was not enough room for everyone to have a seat.

The Young Folks Meeting

In the late afternoon two school buses parked behind the dining tent. Youth from their mid-teens to early twenties got on for the ride to the young folks meeting at a farm several miles away. Linda and Craig found seats with friends from Virginia. Most young people drove to the youth meeting place on their own.

At the farm, the young people made their way to a huge implement shed. At one side of the building sat six young men on a bench behind a folding table. Half of them wore the regulation garb; the others did not. Behind them on the wall was a large sign reading, "Ohio Welcomes You."

The many rows of benches were filled with lively teenagers. Some people, including a number of adults, stood around the edge of the building. Perhaps two-thirds of the young people were dressed in modern clothes, but no shorts were seen on anyone and no girls wore slacks.

Children from Old German Baptist homes did not dress in the church garb until baptism. They could choose to be baptized in early adolescence, or wait until after marriage. Some never became church members.

One of the young men welcomed the group and made a few announcements before introducing the evening speaker. This was a minister who had been especially requested to speak by the host young people. He gave a brief talk encouraging the youth to live for God. After prayer the group was dismissed for supper. A line formed at one end of a long garage and people emerged from the other end carrying plates laden with food. The young folks scattered over the yard, eating where they chose. After supper there were volleyball games at three different locations and softball on a diamond in front of the barn. Activities continued until well after dark.

Pentecost and the Love Feast

Pentecost Sunday, the second day of the meeting, dawned breezy and unseasonably warm. The weather had been dry—a source of worry for the Ohio farmers but pleasant for the rest of the people at the meeting. The mud which sometimes beset annual meeting was absent. Precautions had been taken to avoid a possible slough by planting the entire grounds in grass two years in advance.

The Jamisons came early for a brief worship service and a seven-thirty breakfast. At ten o'clock they were back in the council tent for the main gathering. This morning to accommodate the large crowd there were preaching services simultaneously in two other places—in an implement shed on the meeting grounds and in a nearby Old German Baptist meetinghouse.

The sermons today concentrated on the importance of the Holy Spirit. Isaiah 53 and Acts 2 were read. The Isaiah passage tells of a suffering servant whom Christians believe is Christ, and the Acts chapter describes the outpouring of the Holy Spirit.

Gusts of wind seemed to emphasize the words of Acts 2, verse 2: "And suddenly there came a sound from heaven as of a rushing mighty wind, and it filled all the house where they were sitting." Although the breeze was not especially strong, it was enough to occasionally lift a hat from one of the shelves and land it on some unsuspecting person in the tent.

The Sunday noon meal and afternoon services followed the regular procedure. In the evening there was no supper. Instead, there was a love feast, a special communion observance of Old German Baptists. Other Brethren groups kept this service in slightly different form.

Old German Baptists always sat around tables for love feast, so the observance was held in the dining tent rather than the meeting tent. Because of the limited space in the tent, only a few of the people attending the annual meeting could take part. Even so, the seven hundred people present made for a far larger observance than in a typical congregation.

The tables were covered with white tablecloths. Mark sat in the men's section and Betty and Linda on the women's side. The younger members of the family were away with friends on a local farm.

When all the participants were seated, a hymn was sung. Then a minister rose and read I Corinthians 11, in which Paul describes the proper practice of the Lord's Supper. Several other ministers spoke. Each emphasized that all members should be at peace with God and others, and that they should love the church and desire unity within it. The congregation knelt for prayer.

The period of singing which followed served as a kind of intermission. During the hymns, some four dozen men brought in tubs of warm water, basins and towels. A minister read John 13:1-30, which tells how Jesus washed the disciples' feet. A second minister explained that this act is both an example to be followed literally and a symbol of the inner cleansing which is necessary for participation in communion.

Two men from each table rose and took off their coats (a three-piece suit is always worn at love feast). One of the men took a long towel with apron strings and tied it around the waist of his partner. These two people took a tub of water to the first person in the row facing them. The people in this row had taken off their shoes and stockings. The person who was not wearing a towel stooped down and washed the first person's feet with his hands. He then shook hands with that person, gave him a "holy kiss" and whispered a few words of encouragement. The man with the towel followed, dried the person's feet and greeted him in the same way.

The feet-washing pair repeated the process with a second person, then took their seats. A second pair took over and washed and dried the feet of the next two people in the facing row. After each person finished washing or drying, he went to a small basin at the end of each table and washed his hands with soap and water. When one row had been washed, the roles were reversed and those who had been washed began washing.

The women washed one another's feet at the same time and in the same way as the men.

While this was going on, several Brethren preached about the significance of this practice. It was more important to be washed than to wash, they said. The elder leading the service rose when he thought everyone had been washed and dried and asked if anyone had been missed. The tubs, towels and basins were removed.

There was now a flurry of activity in preparation for the Lord's Supper. Among the Brethren, this observance was quite separate from communion. Eating utensils and cups were quickly distributed by a number of helpers. Water pitchers and bread were also placed at intervals. Bowls of "sop" made from bread pieces soaked in broth and plates of cooked beef were put on the tables.

When all was ready, an elder lined a table hymn and offered a prayer of thanks. All the members reverently ate a portion of the food. Three or four people ate from the same bowl of soup and shared the same cup. When everyone had finished, another hymn was sung and a prayer of thanks was offered.

There was more singing while the tables were cleared. When all had taken their seats again, the ministers of the host districts entered the tent carrying the communion bread and wine. A minister stood and read John 19, which describes Jesus' suffering and death. A second minister gave an intense, moving account of the events described in the chapter.

During this sermon the elder leading the service began breaking the sheets of unleavened bread into long sticks. Each stick had been perforated down its entire length with holes from a fork, to symbolize the wounds of Christ. According to tradition there were five of these.

Five also is the number of times in the New Testament that Christ's followers are instructed to greet one another with a holy kiss, the elder said. He greeted with a kiss the elder seated to his left. This elder in turn greeted the person to his left, and so on around the men's tables until a complete circle was made. The elder walked across the center aisle and shook hands with one of the women. She gave a handshake and kiss to the woman beside her, and so on.

When the salutation was completed, the elder leading the service rose and asked the members to stand while he offered a short prayer of blessing on the bread as he held one of the sticks. At the conclusion of the prayer he quoted from I Corinthians 11: "Take, eat; this is my body which is broken for you." He turned and faced the man on his left. "Beloved brother, the bread which we break is the communion of the body of Christ." He broke off a piece of bread and gave it to the man beside him, who placed the piece on the table. Then he gave the larger piece to him. This next man repeated the same procedure.

The elder then took a piece of bread to the women's side and offered it to the first woman. "Beloved sister, this bread which we break is the communion of the body of Christ." She was given a small piece but not the larger piece to break for the next "sister." Instead the elder again presented the bread to the next woman and to all the communing women. Another elder also served bread on the women's side in order to save time.

When each person had taken a piece of bread, the elder instructed, "Let everyone quietly and reverently partake of this bread, remembering the death of our Savior and what our redemption has cost." Each communicant broke the bread into several pieces and ate it.

When several minutes had passed, the elder rose and poured wine from two different bottles into four cups. This "mingling of the wine" symbolized the members of the church, who were separate yet became one. The elder asked all communicants to stand while he prayed a blessing on the cup. Then he quoted again from I Corinthians 11: "This cup is the new testament in my blood: this do ye as oft as ye drink it, in remembrance of me." He again faced the man to his left. "Beloved brother, this cup of the new testament is the communion of the blood of

Christ." He passed the cup to the man, who took a sip and repeated the same words to the person beside him and so on around the tables. Two elders also gave the cup to each woman. Hymns were sung while the cup was passed, including "Hark! the Sound of Love and Mercy, Sounds Aloud From Calvary."

The elder offered a few remarks, then asked all present to rise while he offered a prayer. The elder in charge of the local congregation made a few comments and announcements and another elder lined a hymn. This marked the end of the love feast. It was a little after ten o'clock, nearly five hours since the beginning of the observance. To many people the evening would have been an ordeal, but to the Old German Baptists it was an exhilarating spiritual experience. Even so, the Jamisons were tired and there was little visiting before a rather short night's sleep.

Business Sessions

The Jamisons stayed with the Clarence Garber family on Sunday night. Both Clarence and Mark were delegates for their respective church districts. Early on Monday morning the two men went to the annual meeting grounds to join other delegates for morning worship and breakfast. All the delegates then went several miles south to the Old German Baptist meetinghouse at Palestine, Ohio.

The first matter to be decided was the selection of the standing committee, the foremost body of authority in the church. The Brethren heard a moving talk about duty from one of the ministers, followed by a prayer asking for the Holy Spirit's guidance. One by one, the delegates filed into the council room and gave their twelve choices to the receiving committee. Delegates also could present any papers stating concerns of their congregations. Each delegate was free to return to the meeting grounds after he had stated his choices.

Following the conclusion of the morning services, the receiving committee spokesman read the names of the twelve elders chosen to the standing committee. Each one announced his presence when his name was called. Then the members of the standing committee went into the farmhouse to select officers: the "foreman" (the term used instead of "moderator" or "chairman"), the reading clerk and the writing clerk.

The committee considered the different papers submitted to the receiving committee and chose subcommittees to respond to the issues raised. The subcommittees went to work immediately, while the standing committee attended to various other matters.

On Tuesday the members of the Old German Baptist Brethren Church gathered at the large council tent for an all-day business session. After a time of singing, the committee led a brief worship service. The reading clerk read chapter 15 from the book of Acts in the New Testament. Another committee member preached on this chapter, which describes how the early church handled controversy.

The foreman conducted the business session. Each subcommittee presented its tentative answer to the queries, then delegates from the congregations that raised the issues and the subcommittee foremen were asked to speak. Afterward the matters were opened for discussion from the floor. The foreman decided when enough had been said and called for a voice vote. The recommendation could be accepted as presented, modified, deferred for a year or rejected. Whatever decision was made applied to all the members of the Old German Baptist Brethren Church.

After all the subcommittees had reported, the reading clerk announced matters related to the permanent committees and other general items. Then the foreman announced the area where next year's annual meeting would be held.

The meeting closed with a song, a few remarks from one of the elders and prayer. This was the official end of the annual meeting, although an evening youth gathering was planned. The Jamisons, like many other families, would stay for that and spend one more night with their hosts before returning home. Annual meeting was always busy and went too fast. There would be much to discuss Wednesday on the way back to Virginia.

6.
Meetings of Other Groups

The annual meeting of the Old German Baptist Brethren is probably the largest gathering of "plain people" in the world. Several plain groups have more members, but none of these churches holds a nationwide conference.

Like other denominations in the Brethren movement, the Old German Baptist Brethren trace their origins to a group of believers who began meeting in 1708 in Schwarzenau, Germany. The heaviest concentration of Old German Baptists is in the Miami Valley of Ohio, where 1,500 members live within a fifty-mile radius. Other large centers are located in northern Indiana and central California.

The largest Brethren group, the Church of the Brethren, has its own annual meeting or conference. Few of the attenders are plain people, however, and the meeting is usually held in a large convention center in a metropolitan area.

The Dunkard Brethren Church, which withdrew from the Church of the Brethren in 1926 over issues including plain dress, also has an annual meeting. This is most often held in camp meeting grounds belonging to other denominations. The annual meetings of smaller Brethren groups do not involve as many days nor as many social aspects as the larger meetings.

Old Order Mennonite groups and some other conservative Mennonites have conferences twice a year, but these are mostly business and policymaking gatherings attended largely by ordained men. The various groups of conservative Mennonites and Beachy Amish have annual fellowship meetings, often at camp meeting grounds. These gatherings are for the purpose of promoting greater unity and scrip-

tural teaching among like-minded groups. Church business is not usually discussed.

Camp meetings and the first camp meeting grounds were not begun by plain people, but by groups identifying with the Holiness movement that sprang from nineteenth century Methodism. However, camp meetings were among many practices of this movement adopted by several groups of plain people. The Brethren in Christ, the United Zion Church and the United Christian Church, which were once considered plain groups, all established camp meetings. Often the older, more conservative members of these groups attend the camp meetings still supported by these churches. The grounds are also rented out to other groups when the governing body is not having its own activities.

Camp meeting grounds are located in rural areas, generally in a grove of trees. There is typically a large, open-sided "tabernacle" for public meetings. There are also facilities for eating and dozens of small cabins. Many people, especially older folks, spend much of the summer at the camp meetings and return year after year to the same cabin. Meetings generally focus on preaching, singing and fellowship with other Christians.

The Old Order Amish do not have large-scale, church sponsored meetings. Each Amish congregation is autonomous, and there is no nationwide church organization or governing body. There are ministers meetings in some communities, in which ordained men from churches recognizing one another as being of the same faith gather to discuss church policy. The Amish of Lancaster County, Pennsylvania, hold these meetings on a regular basis.

Regional Amish School Meetings take on some characteristics of a large religious gathering. The 1987 Ontario/Indiana/Michigan regional meeting held at Aylmer, Ontario, illustrates this. More than 750 people attended this two-day meeting held in a large building occupied by a manufacturer of wood burning stoves. Ministers and other Amish from the various communities presented topics relating to school matters, children and parenting. Titles included "Shaping the Will of the Child Without Breaking the Spirit," "How Parents Should Respond to Teachers' Weaknesses" and "Values in Our Singing." The last topic pointed out the harmful influences of many modern gospel songs, which were written to make money rather than to inspire godliness.

The power of traditional Amish singing was demonstrated when hundreds of voices joined in singing *Wir glauben all an einen Gott* (We all believe in one God). Nearly all the meeting was conducted in the Pennsylvania German dialect. An exception was a quiz for all present, which included multiple choices on the correct pronunciation of English words.

On the second day there were classes for teachers at the three local Amish schools. Non-teachers were invited to a church service at the stove building. A minister from Illinois gave the main sermon.

In addition to Amish from several communities, many Old Order Mennonites from Ontario and Indiana attended the meeting. The Ontario group spoke on "How the Ontario Old Order Mennonite School System Functions."

Other Love Feast Practices

The Old German Baptist Brethren love feast described in Chapter 5 is similar to those of other Brethren groups. The Dunkard Brethren practice is nearly identical, except that grape juice is used instead of wine. Also, at feet washing the same person both washes and dries, and women break the bread to each other instead of an elder breaking bread to each. Some Church of the Brethren congregations still hold the love feast in the old way, but many have ceased to observe feet washing and the Lord's Supper.

The Old Order River Brethren also observe the love feast practice. This group, which originated about 1780 in eastern Pennsylvania, is not related to the other Brethren groups but apparently was highly influenced by them early in its history. River Brethren love feasts are held on a Saturday and Sunday in the spring in most churches. The Lancaster County, Pennsylvania, church also has a love feast in the fall.

Most of the outward forms of the River Brethren are identical to those of the Old German Baptists. The River Brethren, however, do not observe the Lord's Supper (see page 74) but have only the bread and wine. There is no special washing of hands after the feet washing, and the women break the bread to each other. The feet washing is conducted in the double mode (one person washing and another person drying), but the emphasis is on humility and service rather than cleansing. Old Order River Brethren love feasts have traditionally been held in barns, although there have been some exceptions to this practice in recent years. In Lancaster County a school building is often used for love feast.

A unique part of most Old Order River Brethren church services, including love feasts, is a period of testimony called the "experience meeting." At this time both men and women may choose a hymn and tell of God's working in their lives.

7.
An Amish Sunday in LaGrange County, Indiana

Several other buggies were pulling in when Harvey and Edna Bontrager arrived with four of their children at the Alvin Hochstetler farm. The Bontragers' three-mile trip had been a pleasant one on the straight gravel roads of LaGrange County. The sky was clear and the bright sun promised to chase away the chill on this late September morning.

It was eight-thirty when Harvey brought the horse to a stop close to the house. Edna got out of the two-seater black double buggy with baby Vernon and the two girls and went to the door. Susie, eight, and Wilma, four, put their shawls and bonnets on a table on the back porch before going inside.

Ten-year-old Chris rode with his father to the side of the barn. Several buggies were parked in a row near the large, boxy wagon which had been used to transport the wooden benches from the last place of meeting.

Harvey and Chris unhitched the horse and took it to the barn. Harvey met his cousin Joe Bontrager, and the two talked for a few minutes before joining the other men gathered outside the barn. Chris left the adults and found a group of boys his age.

Harvey and Joe said hello to the men individually. As they did so, Harvey made a point to greet each person with a "holy kiss." Harvey found the kiss a meaningful symbol, and he was glad that it was widely practiced in his district. In some of the other districts in the community

it was only practiced by the ministers and a few of the older men.

In keeping with the seriousness considered appropriate before the church service, Harvey and the other men talked quietly among themselves. Eventually the ministers led a group of older men to the house. The others soon followed.

The men entered the house and left their hats on the front porch. They gathered in the living room of the Hochstetler house and found places on the closely spaced backless benches. The boys under twelve came in, and Chris Bontrager rejoined his father.

At the same time, the women took seats in the kitchen and in the downstairs bedroom. Edna chose a place toward the back of the kitchen, since she had a baby. Susie and Wilma sat with their mother and helped care for baby Vernon.

Young children always sat with their parents. Depending on the spacing of the children in individual families, however, some little girls sat with their fathers and some small boys were with their mothers.

A wide doorway between the kitchen and living room marked the boundary between the men's and women's sections. The ordained men sat in a row near the doorway where they could see both groups.

After the adults and children had been seated for a few minutes, the teenage girls filed in as a group and occupied two rows of benches. A little later the teenage boys came in and found their reserved seats. These youth were lined up according to age. The two oldest Bontrager children were with this group: seventeen-year-old Perry and fifteen-year-old Esther. They had come to church separately in Perry's buggy.

Everyone in the house wore Amish garb. The men were dressed in gray or black pants and vests and wore white shirts. The ministers and some of the older men wore frock coats, even though the house was quite warm. All the married men had beards, some quite long. Their hair was cut in bowl fashion. The young unmarried men were clean shaven, and some had haircuts that did not conform to the accepted standard. The young women wore variously colored dresses (shades of solid blue, green and brown), but all of their capes and aprons were white. They also wore black caps that had strings neatly tied beneath their chins.

A few girls were dressed in Amish attire but not in regular church-going clothes. They wore white caps instead of black, and their capes and aprons matched their dresses. They were visiting from other church districts; the regular church garb was encouraged for visitors but not really required. The married women wore white caps and capes, but white aprons were optional. Everyone wore black shoes and stockings, except for the very young children who were barefoot.

The house was now filled to capacity. Most of the regular furniture had been removed so that every bit of floor space could be used. Even so, the 215 people present were almost too many to fit comfortably. For the second time in fifteen years, the church leaders were considering dividing the district. This had been done back in the 1970s, but there had been many marriages and many births since that time. If church services were to be held in the homes of members, the size of each congregation had to be limited.

It was almost nine o'clock when the bishop announced the opening of the service and asked for the first song to be started. Freeman Miller, who was recognized as the song leader, announced the page number of a hymn and asked that David Yoder lead it. Both sat at their regular places while doing so. The people paged through their thick *Ausbund* hymnals to the appropriate place.

The first several notes were for the initial syllable. David sang these solo before everyone joined in on the second syllable. At the beginning of each line the song leader started out in the same way.

While the second line of this song was being sung, the ministers rose and left the room. They went upstairs and met to determine who would take which parts of the service (each of the ordained men took turns). Then they discussed any church business that needed to be taken care of and knelt in prayer.

Meanwhile, the congregation had finished singing the first hymn. The second hymn did not need to be announced; everyone knew it was the Lob Lied, *O Gott Vater Wir Loben Dich* (O Father God, we praise thee). This "praise song" was the second song at every regular service.

A different song leader started this one. "Ooooo-Oo-Ooo-Oo-Oo-Oooo-Ooo," he began before the others joined in on "Gott." The song had four verses and took over fifteen minutes to sing.

After a rather lengthy silence, a young man just learning to lead the singing was asked to lead the third hymn. He was somewhat shaky but managed to get through the first verse. During the second verse the ministers reentered the room and took their seats. The ordained men sat in a particular order that indicated who would take which parts of the service. The singing stopped at the end of the verse.

Minister Abe Miller stood to give the Anfang. Abe was from a church district further south which did not have church this day. He often attended services in this district, because he had a daughter living here.

Abe talked for about half an hour, then asked the congregation to kneel for silent prayer. All present swung around as they descended to the floor and leaned over the benches they had been sitting on. After several minutes the congregation rose to its feet.

Everyone remained standing while deacon Andy Lehman read a

chapter from the New Testament. The men turned to face the speaker, while the women remained facing in the direction they had been kneeling. This scripture reading and the songs that were sung were determined by a schedule followed every year.

A few people left the room while Andy read, including Edna Bontrager, who needed to change baby Vernon. The ministers discouraged exits, but some people considered the scripture reading a convenient time for a break during the three-hour service. Small children needed to be taken care of and mothers often took their babies upstairs for nursing or a nap.

The congregation sat down when the Bible reading was finished, and bishop Levi Yoder stood to preach the main sermon. Levi, fifty-six, was known for his powerful speaking. He handled the German language well and quoted long passages of scripture from memory. Levi used emphatic hand gestures and moved about a great deal. There was no pulpit or speakers stand. The ministers stood on the same level as the rest of the congregation.

Levi tried to divide his eye contact between the men's section and the women's section on either side of the large doorway at which he stood. He did not use the sing-song intonation typical of many Amish preachers but spoke with a strong, clear voice. He was moved with emotion when he spoke to the *yungie leit* (young people). He pleaded with them to live pure lives and seek first the Kingdom of God. He warned of the consequences of careless living and reminded the youth that one reaps what one sows. Some of the young people sat up and paid close attention; others slouched with elbows on knees and heads in hands.

At the end of his sermon, Levi picked up a German New Testament and began reading the second of the specified New Testament chapters for this Sunday. He read several verses at a time and commented on them before continuing.

As Levi spoke, Ida Hochstetler, at whose house the meeting was being held, passed plates of cookies and crackers around to the preschoolers. It was a welcome treat after two hours of sitting.

When Levi finished reading, he sat down and asked minister Moses Lambright to give a response. Moses remained seated and expressed his agreement with the sermon, adding encouragement and warnings of his own. Minister Leroy Mast was invited to "give witness" next. Levi also asked Eli Hershberger to speak since he was visiting from Ohio, even though Eli was not an ordained man.

After the testimonies Levi again stood and said a few words before he asked the congregation to kneel in prayer. This time the prayer was a long, spoken one read from the *Christenpflicht*.

When the prayer ended the congregation rose from its knees but did not sit down. Levi pronounced the benediction. When the name of Jesus was mentioned all bowed their knees slightly.

The congregation sat down and Levi announced at whose home the next church service was to be held. Sometimes a members meeting was held after the regular service, but Levi did not announce one today. The congregation sang a final hymn in the usual Amish manner. When the last notes drifted away, the young men and boys quickly exited row by row. The women and girls did the same.

Chris Bontrager left Harvey's side and went out to be with his friends. Harvey sat and visited but soon had to get out of the way so several men could rearrange benches to prepare for dinner. Tables were constructed by placing two benches in trestle devices which elevated them to the proper level. Women scurried about placing oilcloths on each completed table and making other preparations for the meal. There was one table for the ministers and older men, one for the older women, one for boys and one for girls. Each table seated about twenty people.

It wasn't long until a call was made to come to the tables. When every place was filled, the bishop said that it was time to pray. Heads bowed for a long, silent grace. The bishop cleared his throat slightly to signal the end of the prayer.

The simple meal consisted of bread, butter, various kinds of jam, peanut butter mixed with thick syrup and marshmallow cream, sweet and sour pickles, pickled red beets and cheese. There was water for all and coffee and tea for those who wanted it. Each person had a knife, fork, glass and cup but no plate. The people ate quickly with a minimum of conversation. There would be plenty of time for fellowship after eating. The meal closed with another silent prayer. The people left the tables quickly to make room for the next shift. (There were three different shifts during the afternoon.) Young women rapidly cleaned and reset the tables. Knives and forks were wiped with a damp cloth.

Harvey and Edna both ate at the second seating, but at separate tables. Edna took Vernon and Wilma with her, but the older children had to wait for the third shift.

Harvey went out to the lawn after he ate and found a place on one of the benches that had been placed there. Edna enjoyed chatting with the other women as she helped wash dishes. Susie and her friends helped with the baby.

Families began leaving about two o'clock, but the Bontragers stayed to visit until quarter til three. Harvey and Edna rounded up their four youngest children and went to the buggy. Esther went home with her friend Mattie Miller, and Perry went to the home of Daniel Schrock for a young folks gathering.

When Harvey and Chris got home, they ate popcorn. Then they did the milking and other chores. In the evening Harvey's brother Dennis and his family came for a visit. Edna had not known that company was coming, but she fixed a hot meal for everyone. After supper the children played tag on the lawn.

Perry Bontrager and other members of his young folks group went from the Schrocks' house back to the Hochstetler farm for the evening singing. The Hochstetlers provided a cafeteria-style meal for the group.

About seven-thirty some of the girls began singing at the long table in the living room. More girls came and joined them and the boys took places on the opposite side of the table. Soon both sides of the table were filled. The first songs were from the small German hymnal *Lieder-Sammlung*. Many of the songs had the same words as those used at church services, but the young folks sang them to faster tunes. Later in the evening the group sang English gospel songs from two paperback collections, *Favorite Songs* and *Ninety-eight Selected Songs*.

The singing ended about nine-thirty. The young folks lingered in the house to talk, until one by one the young men went out to hitch up their horses.

The young women got their bonnets and waited outside for their rides home. Some went with their brothers or neighbors, but a few had special friends to take them. Perry Bontrager did not have a girlfriend, but he agreed to take his cousin Frieda Yoder home.

Sunday was over. It was time for another week of work to begin.

Worship Services in Other Amish Communities

The order of Sunday morning church services varies little from one Old Order Amish community to another. But there are other differences.

Perhaps the most obvious of these is the speed of singing. Conservative groups sing slower than the more progressive groups. Among the various Amish groups in Holmes County, Ohio, the Lob Lied or Lobsang may take as long as twenty-five minutes or as little as thirteen minutes.

The tune for the Lob Lied also varies slightly from one community to the next. In some places there are both a fast tune and a slow tune for this song. The Swiss Amish of Adams County, Indiana, have tunes that differ significantly from those of other communities.

The *Ausbund*, which dates back to at least 1564, is the most common hymnal among the Old Order Amish. The *Lieder-Sammlung*, a smaller book published in 1860, is the primary hymnbook in Somerset County, Pennsylvania; Arthur, Illinois; and Kalona, Iowa. The Amish in Daviess County, Indiana, and Aylmer, Ontario, use an 1892 revision of this book.

Customs for prayer, scripture reading and closing announcements also vary. Amish groups at Nappanee, Indiana, and Aylmer have a spoken first prayer instead of the usual silent one. In the nineteenth century immigration communities (Adams, Allen, Daviess and Milverton), the people sit during the scripture reading instead of standing as is customary elsewhere. In Lancaster County the people stand and face backward—in the same direction as they had been kneeling—for the Bible reading and benediction. It is the old custom in Holmes County for the men to turn around while the women face backward. In Lancaster the deacon usually makes the announcements at the end of the church service, while in Ohio and Indiana the bishop performs this function.

All Amish groups have simple after-meeting meals. These usually include bread, butter and spread. In Ohio peanut butter mixed with a sweetener is popular. In Lancaster "snitz" (dried apple pie) is a favorite. In New Wilmington and among the Nebraska Amish, the dried apple pies take the form of a "half moon" turnover. Locally-produced cheese and bologna are often served in Holmes County. The conservative groups (Nebraska, Swartzentruber, Troyer and New Wilmington) serve the traditional bean soup at the meal. Several people eat out of the same bowl.

Old Order Mennonite Services

Worship services of the Old Order Mennonites are very similar to those of the Amish. One of the biggest differences is the Old Order Mennonites' use of meetinghouses. Church buildings are very plain and are furnished with simple benches that have a narrow backrest. The ministers are seated along one of the sides of the building rather than at the end (except in Virginia). In Pennsylvania there is a simple table for the ministers. In Ontario, Indiana and Virginia there is a long boxlike pulpit.

The seating is arranged so that the benches in half the meeting house are parallel to the ministers bench, while those sections to the immediate left and right of the ministers are at right angles. The men's and women's sections are further divided by age and marital status. The men's sections have hat racks along the wall and suspended from the ceiling. There are anterooms for the women to hang their bonnets and wraps; there may or may not be cloakrooms for men. In the Pennsylvania churches the song leaders sit on backless benches at a table which projects at a right angle from the preacher's table. In other groups the song leaders sit with other members of the congregation.

Old Order Mennonites do not have Sunday School. Services usually last between one and a half and two hours. Singing is without instrumental accompaniment. All the horse and buggy groups, except those in Virginia, use German in their services. All Old Order Mennonites who drive cars have switched to English preaching.

Old Order Mennonite groups use small hymnbooks without notes. Unlike the Amish, Old Order Mennonites do not use prayer books or have a schedule for hymns and scripture reading.

Worship services are usually held every other Sunday. In Lancaster County the Wenger and Horning groups share several meetinghouses, taking turns every other Sunday. This is also the practice among the Markham and Woolwich groups in Waterloo County, Ontario.

Plain Brethren Services

Old German Baptist Brethren services are similar to those of Old

The Order of Worship in Old Order Church Services

Woolwich Mennonite
1. Ministers enter
2. Opening hymn
3. Deacon reads scripture
4. Opening sermon
5. Silent prayer
6. Main sermon
7. Comments from other ministers
8. Main speaker responds
9. Audible prayer
10. Closing hymn
11. Benediction (sitting)
12. Announcements

Markham Mennonite
1. German hymn
2. English hymn
3. Opening sermon
4. Silent prayer
5. Deacon reads scripture
6. Main sermon
7. Comments from other ministers
8. Main speaker responds
9. Audible prayer
10. Two songs
11. Benediction (sitting)
12. Announcements

Old Order River Brethren
1. Opening hymn, comments by bishop
2. Deacon requests hymn, makes comments, and leads in prayer
3. Experience meeting (hymns and testimonies from congregation)
4. Bishop closes experience meeting
5. Hymn, opening sermon, prayer
6. Hymn, main sermon
7. Comments by one or more ministers (often preceded by hymns)
8. Closing prayer by last speaker
9. Announcements by deacon
10. Closing hymn (selected by sponsor of meeting)
11. Benediction (sitting)
12. Hymn and prayer for meal
13. Fellowship meal
14. Hymn and prayer after meal

Wenger Mennonite
1. Opening hymn
2. Ministers enter
3. Second hymn (lined by minister)
4. Opening sermon
5. Silent prayer
6. Deacon reads scripture
7. Main sermon
8. Comments from other ministers
9. Main speaker responds
10. Audible prayer
11. Benediction (standing)
12. Closing hymn (lined by minister)
13. Announcements

Horning Mennonite
1. Three or four songs
2. Ministers come in on third or fourth hymn
3. Minister announces remaining hymn and reads the first verse
4. Opening sermon
5. Silent prayer
6. Deacon reads scripture
7. Main sermon
8. Comments from other ministers
9. Main speaker responds
10. Audible prayer
11. Two songs
12. Announcements
13. Benediction (standing)

Old German Baptist
1. Ingathering hymn
2. Main speaker reads from Old Testament
3. Minister requests opening hymn, gives brief sermon, and leads in prayer
4. Deacon reads from New Testament
5. Hymn and main sermon
6. Brief sermons by one or two ministers (often preceded by a hymn)
7. Closing hymn and prayer by last speaker
8. Announcements

Order Mennonites. Contrary to what their name might imply, the Old German Baptists do not use the German language. German Baptists use plain meetinghouses which are arranged much like those of the Old Order Mennonites. There is no raised platform or pulpit. The ministers are seated behind a long table at one side of the meetinghouse, with the deacons on the opposite side of the table. Men and women sit separately, but there is a middle section shared by some of the younger couples, who sit together toward the back of the church.

Old German Baptists kneel for prayer. Some people face forward and others backward. After each prayer a second person prays the Lord's Prayer.

The Old German Baptists use small hymnals that have no musical notation. The minister who selects a hymn "lines" it (see Chapter 5). German Baptist hymn tunes are quite slow in tempo and are designated by meter.

The Old Order River Brethren are often confused with the Old German Baptist Brethren. The two groups are similar in many ways, but have separate origins.

The Old Order River Brethren have not traditionally made use of meetinghouses. Worship services are often held in schools, community centers and other public buildings. In warm weather, meetings are often held in barns.

A noon meal is often part of an Old Order River Brethren service. Until about 1970, people were served at tables in three or more shifts, with a hymn and prayer at the beginning and end of each sitting. This custom is still observed in the two smaller Old Order River Brethren groups. In Lancaster County the fellowship meal is nearly always observed. In other districts it is sometimes omitted.

The River Brethren probably have more singing in their church services than any other Old Order group.

Evangelical Plain Practices

Beginning in the mid-nineteenth century, many plain groups began changing their traditional form of worship and adopting practices from evangelical Protestantism. The Mennonite Church, Church of the Brethren, Brethren in Christ and a large number of Amish churches (called Amish Mennonites) accepted foreign missions, Sunday Schools, prayer meetings, revival meetings, collection plates and gospel songs sung to lively tunes.

The majority of people in these groups wanted to retain plain dress, unsalaried plural ministry and a cappella singing. By the middle of the twentieth century, however, many churches had drifted toward assimilation into the larger society. A minority withdrew from the larger denominations in order to retain traditional practices along with an evangelical church program. The Dunkard Brethren Church, which divided from the Church of the Brethren in 1926, represents this position, as do a dozen or more Mennonite groups that withdrew from the Mennonite Church beginning in the 1950s.

The evangelical plain churches have regularly-scheduled Sunday evening services and prayer meetings. Song books have musical notation and include modern hymns and gospel songs. A song leader usually stands in front of the congregation and beats time in the style of a choral director, but there is no instrumental accompaniment.

Very similar to these groups are the Beachy Amish Mennonites, who separated from the Old Order Amish beginning in the 1920s. They too wanted to blend traditional plain traditions and evangelical worship.

Some Beachy Amish churches have Sunday School every other week, while most have it every Sunday. Only a small number of Beachy churches use German in their church services. Meetinghouses have a raised platform and pulpit for the preachers. A center aisle divides the church into men's and women's sections. This pattern is also followed by groups of conservative Mennonites and Brethren.

8.
A Big Valley Amish Funeral

Amos Yoder's thin beard and long wispy hair blended with the white of the sheets and bolster. His emaciated frame had lain for two days with hardly a movement. The doctor had said yesterday that it would only be a matter of hours. The family had come to witness the departure.

It was ten p.m. The room was illuminated only by two kerosene lamps, and most of the twenty-three people gathered around the bed stood in the shadows. The room was very spartan. The furniture consisted only of a bed, a dresser, a chest and a chair. The walls were white, the woodwork gray. There were no curtains at the windows or carpets on the floor.

Amos's pallid, old face was the focus of everyone's attention. There he lay, his mouth gaping open. Every breath took great effort.

Then the breathing stopped. Hardly anyone in the room exhaled for a few moments. But after an agonizing twenty seconds, Amos's chest began to rise and fall again. Several more pauses in respiration happened within the next several hours. Then, at three-eighteen a.m., the breathing stopped again. Twenty seconds, thirty seconds, a whole minute transpired. No more rasping breaths were heard. Amos was still. His adult sons and daughter stood in silence, grappling with the reality of the moment. Sarah, the youngest of the six children, began to sob. Soon the others were wiping tears. But there was no spouse to grieve. Amos's wife, Susie, had died two years earlier.

When the initial wave of grief subsided, son Joe volunteered to call the family doctor. He went out into the early morning blackness, and

soon the faint light of the lantern on his buggy could be seen moving down the lane.

The family members sat about and talked quietly. The younger grandchildren soon fell into an exhausted sleep. When the adults were able to compose themselves, they began making funeral plans.

Preparations

At five-thirty the headlights of a silver Buick could be seen bouncing down the Yoder lane in the June dawn. The doctor parked among the white-topped buggies and found the path to the door. As he entered the house and peered about the room, the white shirts of the men and white caps of the women stood out in the dimness. One of the men directed the doctor into the next room. The physician went to the bedside and made the usual checks for signs of life. He asked family members a number of questions, made some notes, filled out a few papers and was soon on his way.

By this time funeral arrangements had been worked out. The funeral would be held barely twenty-four hours later, on Thursday morning. There was a certain amount of urgency because the body would not be embalmed.

Two teenage neighbor boys were asked to spread the word about the funeral. The boys broke the news to the closest neighbors as they went about their morning milking. Not all the farms in the valley needed to be contacted. The news spread rapidly among the Amish, up the valley to Belleville and down the valley to Milroy. Telephone messages were sent to non-Amish people in Centre County and Snyder County who had agreed to provide an emergency message service to the Amish communities there.

Meanwhile the undertaker's black station wagon had arrived at the Yoder home. This man would perform only the most minimal of services for the family. The so-called "Nebraska" Amish of Big Valley, Pennsylvania, were the most conservative of the Old Order. When it came to funerals, they were quite self-sufficient. The function of the undertaker was to provide the required link between them and the government—to fill out the necessary papers.

These Amish folk had their own, traditionally-trained people to take care of some of the details of a funeral. Levi and Mattie Speicher would help the Yoders in this way. Levi would see to it that Amos's body was taken care of until the funeral. Because it was summer, special precautions had to be taken to preserve the body since there would be no embalming. The bedroom where Amos lay was closed as tightly as possible. The windows were covered and all the furniture removed. The body was wrapped carefully with a white sheet and laid on a wide board, which was placed lengthwise on a bench. The arms were crossed and tied on the chest. There was no pillow. Every three hours, the body was bathed in alcohol to cool it. A kettle of ice was placed beneath the body, and jars of ice were set at various places on the board close to the corpse.

Relatives, neighbors and friends came to the Yoder home to express their sympathy and offer help. The grieving family did no work. Everyday farm chores were performed by others. Neighbors and church members prepared the meals.

There was no formal viewing before the funeral, but some of the visitors asked to see the body. Levi Speicher accompanied the viewers with a kerosene lamp, then lifted back the sheet to let the people see Amos's face.

When the Yoder family was ready to retire for the night, one of the visitors was asked to have the evening prayer. Not all of the visitors left, however. A number of the young people stayed for the night watch or wake. There was a small meal for the guests at midnight. Levi and Mattie tended to their duties throughout the night.

Service and Burial

A steady stream of white-topped buggies rolled down the Yoder lane, along with a few vehicles with yellow tops and blacks tops from other Amish groups further up the valley. Several vans came with relatives from Centre County and Snyder County, and a few Beachy Amish and Mennonites arrived in cars.

The people took seats on closely spaced benches in the large part of the house, where Amos's son John and his family lived. Women sat on one side of the house, men on the other side. The living room and kitchen were full, but everyone fit; it would not be necessary to hold a second service simultaneously in the barn, as was the practice in case of overflow crowds.

In the bedroom, the immediate family assembled with Amos's body. Here family groups sat together, not men and women separately as was the rule at other gatherings. From this room they could hear the funeral service without leaving the side of the deceased.

Amos's body was dressed and placed in a coffin about an hour before the funeral. He wore a simple white shirt and white pants. A narrow white band about his neck was tied in a simple knot. He had worn this simple tie at his wedding—a practice typical in his generation but less common now.

The coffin was of the traditional shape: wide at the shoulders and narrowing at both ends. The wood was stained dark but was in no way ornamented. There was no lining. The lid was flat; it was slid back to expose Amos's head and shoulders, but the opening would be covered with a white sheet during the funeral service. The coffin was made by a local Amish carpenter, who kept several on hand in various sizes. Coffins had been ordered from the local undertaker until the price got too high.

At ten o'clock, the bishop of Amos's church stood and began speaking. His voice rose and fell in the traditional chant-like manner.

A man of fifty-six, the bishop wore his hair quite long, but his thinning bangs were cut short. His untrimmed beard was a gray-tinged red. Unlike most of the men in attendance, he wore a gray suit. Non-ordained men customarily wore brown suits in Amos's church.

The sermon lasted about an hour. The bishop admonished the people to be ready for death, whether they were old or young. There were words of comfort for the family, but there was no eulogy. Near the end of the sermon, the bishop read from the Gospel of John, chapter 5, verses 24 to 34. This speaks of everlasting life and the passage from death into life. It says that those in the graves will someday hear God's voice. Revelation 20, verses 11 to 15, was also read. This tells of the great white throne of judgment and the book of life.

All knelt for prayer at the end of the sermon, then stood for the benediction. Unlike a usual church service, there was no singing and only one minister spoke. At the very end of the funeral, the bishop stated the age of the deceased. This was the only obituary item mentioned.

The congregation was dismissed, and all but the immediate family went outside while the room was rearranged for the viewing. The four pallbearers and their wives—relatives outside Amos's immediate family—now served refreshments to those in attendance. The two couples who were the most closely related to the deceased served the family in the house. The other two couples served the people standing outside.

The women distributed sweet bread with slices of longhorn cheese on top, while the men carried a tray with two small-stemmed wine glasses and a bottle of wine. They repeatedly refilled the glasses as mourners drank the small amount of wine and returned the glasses to the tray.

The coffin was relocated to the living room. All those in attendance filed past the body. The immediate family members stood behind the coffin, but no one spoke to them or shook hands. After everyone else had viewed the body and gone outside, the family surrounded the coffin and paid their last respects.

When they had finished, the four pallbearers screwed down the lid of the coffin and carried it outside to a waiting spring wagon. This was the simple utility vehicle used by these people. There was no top. Young boys serving as Hostlers had hitched up all the horses of those going to the cemetery and arranged them in the proper order while the viewing was going on.

The simple hearse led the way, driven by Enos Hostetler, a friend of the family. Close family members followed. The procession wound down the lane and continued south on the narrow road which edges the slope of Stone Mountain. The green ridge of Jacks Mountain rose in the distance to the left. The mourners passed fields of knee-high corn and soon-to-be-cut alfalfa. The austere farmsteads of Amos's people dotted the countryside: plain white houses and simple unpainted barns. The long column turned down an even narrower road and soon halted at an enclosed graveyard. The undertaker was present at the cemetery to fulfill the law requiring him to witness the burial.

The drivers tied their horses to the fence. When everyone was assembled in the cemetery, the pallbearers slid the coffin from the wagon and carried it to the grave that they had dug the day before. Beside the new grave was the headstone of Amos's wife, Susie. The marker was small and simple, like all the tombstones in the cemetery. Each grave was arranged so that the feet were toward the east.

Wooden poles had been placed across the hole to rest the coffin on. Two long straps also extended the width of the grave. Each of the pallbearers grabbed an end of one of the straps and pulled up on it, so that the coffin was elevated slightly and the poles could be removed. The coffin was slowly lowered into the grave. At the bottom of the hole was an open-ended, rough wooden box. When the straps were removed, one of the pallbearers climbed down into the hole and placed boards across the width of the box as they were handed to him. After the lid was in place, he was helped out of the hole. The four men began shoveling dirt into the grave as the mourners stood and watched. At first each clump of dirt hit the wood with a soul-jarring thud, but the noise softened as the box was covered with a layer of earth.

After some minutes, the hole was completely filled. All the men removed their hats, and the bishop who had spoken at the funeral conducted a graveside service. There was no singing, but the bishop read a few verses from a hymn. At the end of the ceremony, he invited those present to pray the Lord's Prayer silently.

The mourners climbed into their buggies. Some would return to their homes, others to the Yoder farm, where neighbors and relatives had prepared a meal for all those who wished to partake. Tables were set with potatoes, meat, pork and beans, noodles and fruit pies. Much of the work for this meal had been done the night before.

It would be late in the day before the last of the mourners left the Yoder residence. Many would return the following morning to help get things back in order. The family would divide Amos's belongings, and his end of the house would be used for storage. Eventually John would occupy this end of the house. One generation leaves; another assumes responsibilities. Life goes on in Big Valley.

Funerals in Other Communities

The Amish people described here are the "Nebraska" Amish of central Pennsylvania. Their name comes from the fact that a bishop from Nebraska helped organize the group in 1881. Also known as the "old school" or "white top" Amish (from their white buggy tops), they have retained many customs that have been lost by other Amish groups. A number of funeral practices described in the story are not typical of other Amish communities.

Nearly all Amish groups now agree to have the bodies of their dead embalmed. This is considered more desirable than complying with laws limiting the time between death and burial if embalming is not performed. Without this time limit, relatives living at a distance have more opportunity to attend the funeral.

When embalming was first accepted in Amish communities, the undertaker often came to the home and performed this task. Today the body is usually taken to the funeral parlor for embalming and then returned to the home of the deceased as soon as possible. In Holmes County, Ohio, and adjoining Wayne County, some morticians still do embalming in homes; this is done mostly for the Swartzentruber Amish.

In most cases, the undertaker delivers the body to the home dressed and in the coffin. In Lancaster County the body is dressed in long underwear by the funeral director, and the family members of the same sex dress the body in the funeral clothes. It is also a Lancaster custom for family members to wash the body before the undertaker takes it away.

In Lancaster, males are dressed in a white shirt, white vest and white pants in the coffin. Women are dressed in a white dress and a white cape and apron. Often the cape and apron were worn by the deceased at her wedding.

Like the Lancaster Amish, all the groups in Mifflin County dress the body in white. So do the Amish of New Wilmington, Pennsylvania. In

nearly all other communities, the dead are dressed in their best Sunday clothes: a regular dark suit and a white shirt for men, and a black dress and a white cape and apron for women. In Ohio some older women request to be buried dressed completely in white. Often babies are also buried in white. In the Swiss communities (Adams, Allen and Daviess) women are usually dressed completely in black.

In LaGrange and Adams counties, and often in Holmes, the body is dressed and put in the coffin by the undertaker before being delivered to the home. In Arthur, Illinois, and among the more conservative Amish in Holmes and Geauga counties, the body is placed on a cot provided by the undertaker until a day or less before the funeral. Some people still follow the old custom of not putting the body in the coffin until the morning of the funeral.

In most Amish communities the coffin is placed on simple trestles. The other Mifflin County groups share the Nebraska Amish custom of placing the coffin lengthwise on a bench. The Swartzentruber and Troyer Amish usually place the coffin on two chairs. In Milverton and sometimes in LaGrange, the coffin is placed on an expandable cart device provided by the undertaker.

Coffins are usually made in Amish woodworking shops. All have the same basic shape—wider at the shoulders than at the head and feet—but several details vary from one place to the next. In Holmes, LaGrange and Lancaster, the lid comes to a peak, and the upper section has a two-

part hinged lid that folds back for viewing of the upper part of the body. The Buchanan County Amish use a flat, two-piece lid on their coffins. The Adams County Amish, like members of the Nebraska group, have unlined coffins with flat, one-piece lids. Most Amish coffins have a simple white lining. The Adams County people cover the whole coffin with a white sheet during the funeral. The Lancaster Amish cover the upper part of the coffin with a sheet. In other areas the lid of the coffin is closed during the funeral and has no extra covering. In Arthur, Illinois, Kalona, Iowa, and Hutchinson, Kansas, the coffins have handles along the sides. Nearly everywhere else these are absent.

In Ohio, Indiana and Iowa, redwood is the most common material for coffins, though oak is sometimes used in Ohio and Indiana. Walnut used to be a common material for coffins, before it became scarce. In Lancaster, poplar is the traditional choice.

In Perth and Waterloo counties in Ontario, the Amish and Old Order Mennonites obtain factory-made caskets from the funeral director. These caskets are made of pressed board covered with black cloth and have black handles along the straight sides. (The same style of casket in gray is used for non-Amish paupers.)

The wake or night watch is practiced by the majority of Amish, although this practice has been unknown in Lancaster for many years. It is rare among the Renno group in Mifflin County and the Amish of Kalona, Iowa.

The number of people at a wake varies greatly. In Arthur and Buchanan and LaGrange counties, only two or three people are usually present. The number ranges from four to twelve in Holmes County and from ten to fifteen in Adams County.

Among the Swartzentruber Amish, a group of young folks helps the family of the deceased with farm and household chores. When they are finished with the work, they come to the house and begin singing from the *Lieder-Sammlung* hymnal. This may last until two or three in the morning. Afterward, some of the young people sleep on the floor while at least two stay awake until morning.

In many Amish communities, it is a common practice to hold two funeral services simultaneously for the same person. Usually one service is held in the house and another in the barn or another farm building. This is necessary because of the large number of people who attend—over a thousand in some cases.

In Kalona, Iowa, the Amish often use a large tent for funerals. The Lancaster Amish try to avoid large funerals by limiting the attendance to the local church district and those who are invited.

Sermon and Obituary

The Nebraska, New Wilmington and Adams County Amish have only one preacher speak at a funeral. In other places there are at least two preachers and sometimes three. Typically the first minister speaks on the creation of the world. He points out that Adam was created from dust and each person must return to dust. The first speaker reads John 5:20–30, which speaks of the resurrection of the dead. The second speaker has the main funeral sermon. He reads I Corinthians 15, from verse 35 to the end, including the verse: "O death, where is thy sting? O grave, where is thy victory?" Very little is said about the deceased. The Amish believe that God, not man, should be praised.

The reading of the obituary comes at the end of the service, after the closing prayer and benediction. In most communities the obituary includes the deceased's name, age, date of birth, date of death and number of descendants. Sometimes the names of close relatives are read.

In Lancaster County the minister stands near the coffin during the funeral. In most other places the coffin is in a different room, with the immediate family seated close by. In many communities the mourning family faces toward the coffin, not toward the minister. This custom may be intended to conceal the grief of the family. It is customary in many Amish settlements for the close relatives of the deceased to sit together in family groups, rather than men and women separately as at other services.

In Holmes County a small group of people may sing just before the viewing. This group usually consists of older men who normally lead singing and girls in their early teens who have been asked to serve at the funeral meal. The songs are usually not the slow church tunes but slightly more modern melodies. In LaGrange a group sometimes sings during the viewing.

In most cases the coffin is not moved for the viewing, although in Ohio and Indiana it is sometimes taken outside. Among groups other than the Nebraska Amish, relatives usually sit while the other people view.

The closest family members always view last at an Amish funeral. Usually the coffin maker decides when they have had sufficient time for this final viewing. It is the coffin maker's job to screw down the lid of the coffin.

The hearse takes the form of an open spring wagon in all the groups in Mifflin County. This is also the type of vehicle used by the Swartzentruber and Troyer Amish, and by the Amish of Adams, Allen and Milverton, who use open vehicles for all purposes. The Amish in Holmes and LaGrange counties and elsewhere have vehicles with an open bed and an enclosed driver's seat that serve as hearses. A black oilcloth cover is put on the coffin for the drive to the cemetery. In Lancaster County a special enclosed hearse is used. This looks much like a Lancaster market wagon, except the top is black instead of gray.

Graveside Practices

The Milverton, Arthur and Lancaster Amish have a final viewing at the cemetery before burial. This is also sometimes practiced in Geauga County.

The rough box into which the coffin is placed in the grave takes one of two forms. Most boxes are like those described for the Nebraska Amish: wooden frames onto which individual pieces of wood are laid for a lid. There are two or three pieces of wood across the bottom for the coffin to rest on, so that the lowering straps may be removed. In Lancaster, LaGrange, Arthur and Buchanan, the box has a lid that is nailed together and lowered into the grave like the coffin.

In Arthur as well as Holmes, Geauga and LaGrange counties, a men's group sings while the grave is filled by the pallbearers. The bishop in charge reads a hymn, several lines at a time, and the singing group follows. One hymn usually lasts until the grave is full. In Kalona, Iowa, a group of young people sings at the graveside. In Lancaster and Mifflin, the bishop begins reading a hymn when the grave is half full and continues until the job is finished. There is no singing.

It is the usual Amish custom for the bishop to ask the congregation to pray the Lord's Prayer silently at the conclusion of the graveside service. In Adams County the minister does not speak until the grave is completely full. He then says a few words and has an audible prayer. In most communities the men remove their hats when the minister speaks; in Adams they do so only for the prayer. In Kalona the men take off their hats when they enter the cemetery. It is also the Kalona practice for the minister to speak when the grave is level full. The pallbearers finish the job after the people have left.

In most Amish communities there are four pallbearers; in Kalona there are six. These are normally neighbors and friends, but in Lancaster they may be grandsons, cousins or nephews. In Adams, Lancaster and Mifflin the pallbearers shovel two at a time and trade off when they tire. In most other places the four men are replaced by four others after the grave is half full. In Holmes County the youngest pallbearer is the one who gets into the grave and places the top on the rough box. In Milverton the pallbearers do not dig the grave. This is taken care of by young men in the community.

The meal after the funeral is usually very simple. In Holmes County bread, butter, beets, pickles and coffee are served. Cheese, bologna and sometimes cake or cookies are added to this menu in Adams County, and lettuce and pie in Buchanan. In Geauga sandwiches and noodles are typical. Often in LaGrange a prepared tray of food is provided, which might include two hot dishes.

Cemetery plots are usually arranged according to family groupings. In Holmes County there are small, family cemeteries scattered through the hilly countryside. In other communities the cemeteries are more consolidated. In Adams and Milverton there are separate rows for adults, children and infants, and the burials are made in the order of death. This is probably a carry-over from the limited space available for cemeteries in Europe.

Grave markers in Amish cemeteries are generally small and plain. Many are made of cement, though more substantial stones of marble, granite and sandstone are used widely. The Adams County Amish have only narrow wooden markers, most of which carry no name. The location of graves is recorded in a small book. The Milverton Amish have simple cement markers often bearing only the initials of the deceased.

Old Order Mennonite Funerals

The Old Order Mennonites have funeral customs much different from those of the Amish. The Wenger Mennonites use the same kind of coffins as the Amish, but the bodies are dressed in shrouds—long, white, gown-like garments for men and women. Women's shrouds have capes.

The first part of an Old Order Mennonite funeral takes place at the home of the deceased. Here a short service is held for the close family members. Then the coffin is put in a hearse and transported to the cemetery, usually located beside the meetinghouse. The coffin is put on trestles outside and a large crowd views the body. Males file by on one side and females on the other. The immediate family views last. The coffin is taken to the grave and lowered into the rough box. The minister preaches a brief sermon, and a hymn is usually sung while the grave is filled in.

After the burial, the people gather in the meetinghouse for the funeral service. This follows the general pattern of a regular church service and lasts one and a half to two hours. Some of the people return to the home for a meal after the funeral.

Horning Mennonite funerals are very much like those of the Wenger Mennonites. Coffins and shrouds are used, and the sequence of events is the same. One of the few differences is that Horning coffins have handles on the sides.

The Old German Baptist Brethren have their viewings at funeral homes. On the morning of the funeral, a brief service is held at the funeral home for the immediate family. The body is then taken to the church and placed in front of the assembly room. The casket remains closed during the funeral sermon. The casket is opened after the service and the mourners file by the casket for a final viewing. A meal is served in the church basement after the burial. Nearly all German Baptists use conventional caskets rather than coffins, and traditional white shrouds are rare.

Among the Old Order River Brethren, shrouds and old style coffins are still occasionally used, but conventional graveclothes and caskets are more typical. A tent and modern lowering devices are usually used at the cemetery. Viewings may be in the home of the deceased or at a funeral home. River Brethren funerals are often held in the churches of other denominations or at a school owned by the group in Lancaster County. There is usually a viewing before the funeral but not after. The funeral service lasts about one and a half hours, with several ministers taking part. The Old Order River Brethren do not have their own cemeteries.

9.
The Auction at Bart

The traffic jam started about a mile from Georgetown. The Stoltzfus family had rolled along quite rapidly in their carriage over the hilly terrain south of Paradise, but now as they approached the sale grounds the traffic was bumper to bumper. Or rather nose to bumper, in the case of the Stoltzfus buggy. Several of the properties along the road had No Parking signs posted, but father Jacob knew of a place where their horse and buggy would be welcome. Several Amish families on the outskirts of this small village provided parking places for the many Amish people who came to the big sale.

Jacob pulled into the lane and let Becky and the children off before finding a place for his carriage among the tightly packed rows of gray vehicles. The seven Stoltzfuses joined a stream of people making their way to the sale grounds. Other streams of plainly clad folk flowed from other directions and met in a virtual flood of black hats, bonnets and shawls at the Bart Township Fire Company. Hundreds, even thousands of Amish people covered the several acres of the sale grounds. Scattered here and there among the black garbed plain folk like candy sprinkles on the top of a cupcake were more colorfully dressed "English" neighbors.

This sale, held every March, was Lancaster County's closest equivalent to an Amish fair. The Amish forbade participation in real fairs because of the events' frivolity and competition, but the Bart sale and the similar Gordonville auction were considered different. Their purpose was to raise money to benefit the fire companies, as well as to provide places for Amish people to buy and sell items unique to their needs.

Jacob and his sons Joe, seventeen, and Levi, ten, separated from Becky and the three girls: Suvilla, fifteen; Ruth, twelve; and Katie, seven. Jacob stood in line for a buyer's number, while the boys looked at

stacks of lumber.

Becky and the girls wandered through the rows of furniture that were lined up near a small block building. Katie wanted a small school desk. But their main interest was the quilts in the main fire hall.

Becky looked in her bag to see what her number was. The card said 275. The Stoltzfuses had only brought their quilt to the fire hall on Thursday, so they had a high number. The quilts would be sold in the order in which they had been brought.

Ruth raced ahead and was the first to locate their quilt on the rack. It was a queen-size log cabin pattern using a barnraising variation. Becky had spent many winter hours stitching the piece. Suvilla had also helped a great deal since she was no longer in school.

As they looked at their quilt and those around it, an elderly Amish woman approached Becky. "Are you Abe's Levi's Katie?" she asked.

"No, I'm Abe's Levi's Becky. Redbeet Sam's Jake is my husband."

"Oh yes, Redbeet Sam's Lizzie married my brother's boy, Ben."

"Then you must be Hog John's Annie."

"Yesss," the older woman squealed, and the two continued their genealogy game.

Suvilla and Ruth left their mother and Katie and found their own circle of friends. Neither was old enough to belong to one of the young people's groups, but they did gravitate toward Amish of similar age and convictions. Becky insisted that her girls wear shawls and bonnets, and Suvilla and Ruth tended to congregate with girls who dressed the same. Some other groups of girls standing in little groups around the sale grounds were dressed less conservatively. They did not wear bonnets or shawls, and their coats had ornamental pins on the lapels. Their dresses were short by Amish standards, and thin stockings and running shoes adorned their feet rather than the traditional black oxfords.

In back of the fire hall, women and girls in a variety of attire flocked around a parked truck. Here a wavy haired man assisted by a tall black man displayed volumes of yard goods. In a loud voice he told of the qualities of each. Suvilla had her eye on a bolt of royal blue fabric. She thought it would be nice for her first singing, which would be coming up after her soon-to-be-observed sixteenth birthday.

Over in the rows of farm machinery, Jacob, Joe and Levi studied a corn binder. It looked to be in excellent shape, but the rubber tires would need to be replaced with steel wheels in accordance with Amish beliefs. Close by, a crowd of men encircled an ancient McCormick Deering tractor. The owner cranked it to a sputtering start to demonstrate that it still ran, and the auctioneer rattled off his staccato spiel, drawing out bids from the crowd. The machine went to an antique tractor collector, who outbid an Amishman who had intended to use it for belt power on his farm.

A blaring voice announced that the horses and mules would be sold in an hour. The boys looked at their pocket watches and hoped that the corn binder would be their father's by then. The auctioneer worked his way down the line of equipment, some of it old and rusty, some of it brand new, until he reached the desired item. The owner, a stocky ruddy faced man with a red and white Purina cap, told the group that it was in good working order. He had brought it from his farm in York County, knowing the Amish demand for otherwise obsolete machinery.

"Who'll give two hundred dollars?" the auctioneer shouted. No one bid. "A hundred, who'll give a hundred?" There were still no takers.

"Fifty," Jacob spoke out.

Now the auctioneer shifted into high gear and chattered like a stick dragging on the spokes of a turning wheel. He got a bid of seventy-five from another man and turned to Jacob, asking for a hundred. Jacob nodded confidently. One hundred twenty-five, one hundred fifty, two hundred. Jacob's nods came more slowly. The auctioneer's helper, a short wiry Amishman, assisted in spotting bids. Occasionally when he saw a bid he yelped in a high pitched voice sounding like a dog having its tail stepped on. He sometimes even jumped into the air. This never failed to draw chuckles from the crowd.

The price had now reached five hundred dollars. Only Jacob and another Amish farmer were bidding. Jacob nodded at five hundred fifty. The auctioneer turned to the other bidder. "Six hundred, g'me six hundred." The man shook his head. "Five seventy-five, five seventy-five, five seventy-five." The auctioneer scanned the crowd for other bidders. "Sold for five hundred fifty dollars," he said, pointing to Jacob. Jacob quickly withdrew his bidders number from his inside coat pocket and held it up so the large black number could be seen. "Number 767," the auctioneer said to the clerk, who stood nearby with a clipboard recording item numbers, buyer numbers and prices.

Jacob sighed deeply. The two boys looked at each other and smiled broadly. They lingered to take another look at their new possession, as the crowd moved on down the long rows of plows, spring tooth harrows, corn planters, grain drills, side delivery rakes and silo fillers. Jacob, Joe and Levi watched from a distance as a large old hay loader was carefully examined by two Amishmen dressed in blue coats and pants in contrast to the usual Lancaster County black. They were from Dover, Delaware, where these old style machines were used rather than the motorized hay bailers used in Lancaster.

The trio made their way to the long row of buggies, carriages, wagons and sleighs at the very back of the sale grounds. They really didn't have a need for any vehicles but it was still interesting to look.

Jacob saw his cousin Jonas from Kirkwood, and the two caught up on family and local news. Joe and Levi moved on to the horse barn. The boys found two rows of steeds hitched along the walls, from a small pinto pony to a team of huge Belgians. Canny horsemen scrutinized the traits of each animal.

Levi and Joe went outside and found a place along the roped off area extending from the barn. One by one the horses were led out to be sold. Enthusiastic young boys gave the animals a good run around the ring, with the horses kicking up dirt when making a sharp turn. The Stoltzfus boys watched for half an hour, then decided it was time to eat.

At the fire hall, Joe and Levi had to wait their turn in the shoulder-to-shoulder crowd. Dozens of Amish women scurried about behind the tables, frantically filling orders. The boys got their subs and chicken corn soup and went outside to wolf them down.

Along the street the boys saw a row of trucks filled with hay. This too would be auctioned off. But of greater interest to Levi and Joe was a flurry of activity across the street. A large group of boys and girls were gathered at a fenced-in area. Joe and Levi found a vigorous game of corner ball going on, with four boys positioned at the corners of a large square. More boys were huddled within the square. The boys at the corner threw a small ball (about the size of a baseball but not quite as hard) back and forth rapidly to one another. The boys in the middle cautiously eyed each flight of the sphere. Suddenly the ball whizzed into the center and clouted one of the boys, who fell to the ground trying to avoid the impact. He dusted himself off dejectedly, picked up his hat and shuffled out of the square. The process went on until only one boy was left in the center. With flexed knees and quick jerks of the neck he watched the path of the ball, skillfully dodging, diving and stepping aside when the ball was targeted at him. Then in a quick maneuver he too was hit in the back. The corner men and others went to the middle, and the game started again.

Becky and Katie, who had been rejoined by Suvilla and Ruth, stood in the crowd around the end of the fire hall. They had watched for more than an hour and a half as the quilts were sold one by one. Each quilt was conveyed to the auction stand by a pulley-controlled cable.

Although the Stoltzfuses enjoyed seeing all the quilts, their hearts beat faster when their own quilt appeared. Becky was afraid that it would not bring a good price, coming so late in the sale. She and Suvilla glanced at each other nervously as the bidding started slowly. Gradually the pace quickened. The price went up to two hundred dollars, and all but two bidders were eliminated. One was a tall light-haired woman with a leather jacket and long red fingernails, the other a plump elderly

lady with a fur-collar coat. At four hundred dollars, the bidding slowed. The price made twenty-five dollar jumps to five hundred fifty. At five hundred eighty dollars, the elderly woman dropped out. The tall woman rushed to pick up her precious bundle. "It was the only one that matched my bedroom!" she exclaimed to no one in particular.

Becky and the girls were elated. It would have been out of Amish character to celebrate visibly, but they certainly did so on the inside. They would receive a handsome commission for their work, and the fire company would get needed funds.

After the quilt was sold, Suvilla and Ruth joined the boys at the corner ball game and shared a bag of candy with them. The four of them observed the action for some time until approached by their parents and Katie. Jacob was carrying a chair and an axe, Becky had a bundle of fabric and a step stool, and Katie clutched a kerosene lantern. The older children relieved their parents of their loads and reluctantly walked to the buggy for the trip home.

Other Sales

Public sales or auctions are very important social events in the plain communities. These occasions take the place of many forms of enter-

tainment enjoyed by the larger society. Farm sales are held sporadically in all communities, usually in the winter and early spring. On these occasions the goods of those who are moving, retiring or deceased are auctioned off. Sales are also held to provide for special needs in the community, such as large medical bills. In many communities, sales are held as fund-raisers for schools or fire companies, like the one at Bart.

The Mennonite Central Committee (MCC) holds auctions in many locations throughout the United States and Canada to raise money for worldwide relief work. These sales feature quilts donated by dozens of sewing circles, as well as a wide variety of other items. The MCC sale at Harrisburg, Pennsylvania, attracts people from all branches of the Anabaptist family, plain and non-plain, as well as many other people who are interested in fine handicrafts.

In many communities of plain people, as in other rural areas, there are sale barns where farmers bring their livestock to be auctioned off. These large buildings usually have amphitheater-type seating that funnels down to a show area through which the animals are led. The sale barn at New Holland, Pennsylvania, is larger than most and has a special area for horses, which are sold every Monday.

Other activities often accompany these community livestock sales, such as the produce market and flea market at Belleville, Pennsylvania, and the large machinery sales held at Kidron, Ohio, which are on the same scale as the sale at Bart. There are also community farmers markets that are heavily patronized by plain people, including Green Dragon and Root's in Lancaster County, Peddlers Village near Goshen, Indiana, and Spence's Bazaar at Dover, Delaware. On a larger scale is the sale and flea market at Shipshewana, Indiana. This has grown to be much more than a distinctively Amish event. Several farmers markets in Lancaster County and in Waterloo County, Ontario, cater mainly to non-plain people, but Amish and Old Order Mennonites maintain many of the stands.

10.
Holidays, Family Days and Working Days

The Old Order people recognize nine or more special days during the year. The majority of these days are observed in a very limited way, however, with no elaborate festivities and few quaint customs.

Christmas

As in the larger society, Christmas is the most cherished of holidays. However, very few of the trappings usually associated with this day are found among the plain people. Decorated trees, mistletoe, Santa Claus and the like are noticeably absent. The leaders of the Old Order churches try to direct their members' attention to the importance of Christ's coming to earth and away from the worldly Yultide festivities.

Parents and grandparents do not inundate their children with Christmas presents, but in most communities some gift-giving is considered appropriate. Clothing, books, farm-related toys, plainly dressed dolls and table games are typical gifts. Teenage girls often receive items for their hope chests. Dating couples also exchange gifts at Christmas. If the couple is quite serious, the boy might give his girl-friend china, silverware or a clock.

Because of the large size of many extended Old Order families, it is often impractical to give gifts to each family member. Individuals draw names from a hat and present gifts to the selected person at the family Christmas gathering.

The Christmas dinner is the most important holiday celebration in

Old Order groups. Each family is usually involved in several such gatherings, and the conflicting schedules of in-laws may make it necessary to extend the holiday season well beyond its usual limits; "Christmas" dinners might even be held in February. Besides family gatherings there are dinners for groups of friends from teenage years, gatherings for single women, get-togethers for teachers, events for parents of children going to the same school and so on.

During the holiday season, women often gather to make cookies together. Children and youth often go Christmas caroling.

Food at Christmas gatherings is much like the rich fare of wedding feasts: roast fowl, stuffing, mashed potatoes, vegetables, pickled relishes, pie and lots of cookies and candy.

Although they do not use colored lights or tinsel, Old Order families sometimes decorate their houses with greens and candles. Schoolchildren might provide decorations made at school, and a string of Christmas cards could be displayed for ornamentation.

Many Old Order schools have special Christmas programs. These usually consist of Christmas songs in both German and English and recitations by students. Some schools also have skits, but these are frowned upon in many areas.

The religious observance of Christmas is, of course, paramount to the Old Order people. The Old Order Mennonites always have church services on Christmas Day. The Old Order Amish may or may not have church on Christmas, depending on which day of the week Christmas falls. In Lancaster County, if Christmas Day comes during the beginning of the week no church service is held on the actual day, but if it comes toward the end of the week there is church on Christmas. The Christmas church service follows the same format as a regular Sunday morning service, but the importance of Christ's birth is emphasized.

The Old Order Amish in Ohio traditionally put more importance on "Old" Christmas—January 6—than on "New" Christmas—December 25. In Ohio no work is done on either day, but only Old Christmas is observed as a fast day.

In larger Christendom, January 6 is called Epiphany and recognized as the day the three wise men visited the Christ child (or the day Christ was baptized, or the wedding was held at Cana or the four thousand were fed). The Amish do not make any of these associations, but observe the day because it was the original date of Christmas before the change from the Julian to the Gregorian calendar.

In Lancaster County, January 6 is not recognized as a holiday at all. Instead, the Amish there observe December 26 as "Second Christmas." This is primarily a day of visiting and a break from one's usual work. All Amish shops are closed, but many Amish go shopping in non-Amish stores. Easter Monday and Pentecost Monday are observed in much the same way. (Fishing is a favorite activity on Pentecost Monday.)

Other Holidays

Easter receives special emphasis in church, but few other customs or practices are associated with the day. Some families color eggs, but the Easter Bunny is rarely mentioned.

The Easter season is commemorated with a communion service in most Old Order groups, though this is not always held on Easter Sunday. Good Friday is set aside as a prayer and fast day.

Ascension Day, which always falls on a Thursday, is observed with a church service among Old Order Mennonites and in some Old Order Amish communities. In Holmes County it is a fast day; in Lancaster it is generally not. Pentecost is given special emphasis at church. The Old German Baptist Brethren and related groups have their annual Conference around Pentecost.

The Lancaster County Amish observe October 11 as a fast and prayer day preceding communion. This is St. Michael's Day, but the Amish do not venerate St. Michael or even know who he was.

Old German Baptist Brethren and many Old Order Mennonites have regularly scheduled church services on Thanksgiving. The Amish in Holmes County, Ohio, have adopted Thanksgiving as a prayer and fast day, and do not work. In Lancaster County, Thanksgiving is swallowed up by the wedding season. Some Old Orders in the United States do not recognize Thanksgiving as a valid holiday, since it was established by the U.S. government. Others say that one should be equally thankful every day.

In late summer or sometime in autumn, Old Order Mennonites in Virginia, Indiana and Ontario and Old Order River Brethren have harvest meetings. These gatherings are to give thanks for the bounties of the land and spiritual blessings. The scripture reading schedules of the Old Order Amish commemorate various points in the agricultural cycle: *Säeman*—planting or sowing—in April, and *Ernte*—harvest—and *Einsammlung*—ingathering, both in July.

Near the end of the year the Amish read Matthew 24 and 25 at a designated church service. The tribulation and deception of the Last Days are prophesied in these chapters, which are called the *Weltende* or end of the world scriptures.

New Year's Day causes little ado in Amish circles, though the passing of another milestone in life's journey is noted. There are generally no special church services on New Year's Day, though the young folks in some groups may get together for an evening program.

Because of their military connotations, U.S. Independence Day, Veteran's Day and Memorial Day are not recognized by the plain people. Labor Day passes unnoticed, and Halloween is not observed. Mother's Day and Father's Day receive some attention depending on the group and individual family.

Working Days

The Old Order people modify a common maxim to say, "The family that *works* together stays together." This same attitude is extended to the church and community. Working together to accomplish a given task is considered the best way to build cohesiveness in the Christian community. Times of work are times one can show concern for a sister or brother in the church, and give the person receiving help a feeling of love and closeness to the group. Some people believe that one of the reasons the Old Orders limit technology is to provide more opportunities to work together.

Within families, "Sisters Days" are common in Old Order Communities. Sisters from the same family (there are half a dozen or more in many cases) gather in one of the siblings' homes. They spend the day sewing, canning, cleaning or doing some other domestic task.

Quilting bees are a major social event among Old Order women. These can be sisterly functions, but often include other relatives as well as neighbors and friends.

To the plain people the word "frolic" does not denote frivolity. Instead, it means a "work party." To Old Order people, work is fun, especially with a large group of people. The best known and largest scale frolic is the barn-raising. When fire strikes or a new farm is established, hundreds of people gather to construct a gigantic barn in as little as one day. Women do not take part in actual construction, but provide a sumptuous meal for the workers. All the labor is free. In the case of a natural calamity, the church pays for some or all of the building materials. The recipient returns the favor by helping at other barn-raisings. Smaller building frolics are also held to erect various other farm structures.

Husking bees are still held in a few Old Order communities where corn is still put in shocks. Apple butter frolics that produce gallons of sweet, brown spread are still common, as are butchering frolics which provide for a family's needs of beef or pork.

Threshing wheat in early July is often a group effort. The purchase and upkeep of a threshing rig is usually shared by a group of farmers known as a threshing ring. These men also help with the work involved as the threshing machine is brought to each farm. The day includes a hearty thresherman's dinner.

Silo filling also is often a joint effort among a group of farmers.

In late summer, families gather at one-room schoolhouses to make preparations for the new school year. Floors are swept, windows washed and desks scrubbed. The workers also tidy up the grounds and make necessary repairs. At the end of the school year, the parents of the students gather again—this time for an old fashioned picnic with games that involve children and parents alike.

Reunions

Some Old Order gatherings do not involve either the celebration of a religious holiday or the accomplishment of a given task. Large-scale family reunions take place in the summer. Some of these are highly organized affairs with programs and speakers. Hundreds of people may attend. Such reunions are primarily for those who are interested in genealogy or *Freundschaft*. The actual relationships between the attenders identifying with a certain surname might be rather remote. Many of the participants are not members of one of the plain churches. The Old Order Mennonites have discouraged attendance at these gatherings because of the frivolity that was associated with reunions around the turn of the century, when they gained popularity.

Old Order Mennonites also have discouraged surprise parties. Birthday celebrations are usually simple affairs in Old Order families. Cakes with candles are generally absent in the more conservative churches, but homemade ice cream is a frequent birthday treat. Children receive some gifts, and "Happy Birthday" is sung at school. Special birthday gifts between girlfriends and boyfriends are usual.

There are also a number of gatherings which bring together people who are involved in certain occupations. These include buggy-making, harness-making and pallet-making. There is generally no organized program at these meetings, but time is provided to compare notes on methods, supplies and outlets.

A very large annual meeting of Old Order handicapped people is held at varying places across North America. In the early years of these meetings the handicapped were often outnumbered by other visitors. This necessitated limiting the attendance to the handicapped and those who might be needed to help them.

About the Plain Groups

The Amish, along with certain Mennonite and Brethren groups, make up the plain people. In addition to plain dress, all of these groups share the doctrines of adult believers baptism and nonresistance (a form of pacifism). All emphasize separation from the world, though many differences have arisen over where to draw the line between church and world.

The Amish

The Old Order Amish are the largest and most conservative group of plain people. The Amish church began in 1693, when the followers of Jacob Amman divided from the Mennonites in Switzerland, Alsace and Germany, in order to implement stricter church discipline. The Amish began immigrating to America in the eighteenth century and eventually died out as a separate group in Europe.

During the last half of the nineteenth century, a great rift developed among the Amish. The progressives were absorbed into the Mennonite Church, while those who retained the old traditions became known as Old Order Amish.

The Amish have a total population of about 100,000. About half this number are baptized church members. The largest concentrations of Old Order Amish are in Ohio, Pennsylvania and Indiana. There are also settlements in seventeen other states and in Ontario, Canada.

Beginning in the 1920s, the Beachy Amish (named after a leader, Moses Beachy) withdrew from the Old Order Amish. These people wished to keep plain dress but at the same time accept modern technology and an evangelical church program. The Beachys and related groups have approximately 7,000 members.

Mennonites

The Mennonites began in Switzerland in 1525 as a part of the Anabaptist movement. A similar group started a few years later in the Netherlands. Both groups eventually were named after a prominent Dutch leader, Menno Simons.

Due to severe persecution in Europe, Mennonites came to North America in large numbers in the early 1700s. Settlements were first established in Pennsylvania and soon spread to the north, south and west.

By the middle of the nineteenth century, Mennonites were being heavily influenced by evangelical Protestantism. Those members who feared a loss of the church's traditional ways withdrew to form Old Order Mennonite groups. Old Order churches were begun in Pennsyl-

Major Old Order Communities

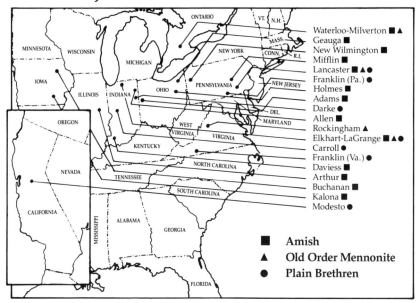

Waterloo-Milverton ■ ▲
Geauga ■
New Wilmington ■
Mifflin ■
Lancaster ■ ▲ ●
Franklin (Pa.) ●
Holmes ■
Adams ■
Darke ●
Allen ■
Rockingham ▲
Elkhart-LaGrange ■ ▲ ●
Carroll ●
Franklin (Va.) ●
Daviess ■
Arthur ■
Buchanan ■
Kalona ■
Modesto ●

■ Amish
▲ Old Order Mennonite
● Plain Brethren

vania, Ontario, Ohio, Indiana and Virginia.

During the second quarter of the twentieth century, the Old Order Mennonite communities experienced another set of divisions. At this time, the more progressive groups adopted cars and the use of English in their church services.

The horse and buggy Old Order Mennonites have over 6,000 members. There are about 5,000 members of the car-driving groups. The total population of each group is about double the membership.

The largest conservative Mennonite groups formed in the 1950s over concern that the Mennonite Church was becoming assimilated into the larger society. Though the breakaway groups appreciated the evangelical emphasis of the church, they wanted to retain a degree of separation from the world in dress and lifestyle. These fellowships have some 13,000 members.

Brethren

The Brethren movement began in 1708 in Schwarzenau, Germany. In most respects the Brethren had the same tenets of faith as the Mennonites, and the early Brethren considered themselves an Anabaptist renewal movement. The major difference between Mennonites and Brethren was mode of baptism. The Brethren immersed, the Mennonites poured. It was from their practice of trine immersion that the Brethren received the names "Dunker" and "Dunkard."

Brethren immigrated to North America soon after the movement started, and their numbers grew very rapidly in the New World. Soon the Brethren were the largest plain group.

By the early twentieth century, the majority of Brethren had adopted modern ways. An Old Order minority withdrew from the larger body (later known as the Church of the Brethren) in 1881. This group took the name Old German Baptist Brethren. Currently it has some 5,000 members in sixteen states.

A second conservative group withdrew from the Church of the Brethren in 1926 to become the Dunkard Brethren Church. This "evangelical" plain group has a little over a thousand members in thirteen states.

The River Brethren began quite separately from the larger Brethren movement. The River Brethren combined Mennonite, Brethren and German revivalist influences. They got their name because the first members lived near the Susquehanna River in Pennsylvania.

As in other plain groups, tensions between progressive and traditional River Brethren developed in the nineteenth century. A conservative minority withdrew from the progressive majority (now the Brethren in Christ Church) in the 1850s. The Old Order River Brethren have some 300 members in Pennsylvania and Iowa.

Afterword

The stories in this book are fictional but depict typical happenings in actual communities. The actions and thoughts of the characters show the values upheld by the communities portrayed. Admittedly, not all individuals in the groups live up to these expectations. There are varying levels of Christian commitment even among the plain people.

Names used in the book are fictional but are characteristic of the communities described. Each Old Order community has a peculiar set of names, both first and last. Many of the place names mentioned are real, but the names of church districts, congregations and young people's groups are fictional.

Though tradition governs most aspects of the observances depicted, many variations in minor details can occur. It is impossible to list all of these. The chapters and parts of chapters that discuss variations are meant to suggest the diversity that exists among plain groups, not to provide an exhaustive analysis.

Most of the information for this book was obtained from members of the Old Order communities, through interviews, letters, questionnaires and direct observation. Some secondary sources were consulted, but information from them was verified by Old Order people.

Readings and Sources

Books

Bachman, Calvin George. *The Old Order Amish of Lancaster County.* Norristown, Pennsylvania: Pennsylvania German Society, 1941, 1961.

Benedict, Fred W. *The Brethren Love Feast.* Pendleton, Indiana: Old Brotherhood Publishers, n.d.

Christenpflicht. Scottdale, Pennsylvania: Mennonite Publishing House, 1986. The most commonly used prayerbook among the Amish.

Durnbaugh, Donald, ed. *The Brethren Encyclopedia.* Oak Brook, Illinois and Philadelphia: The Brethren Encyclopedia, Inc., 1983.

Dyck, Cornelius J., ed. *An Introduction to Mennonite History.* Scottdale, Pennsylvania: Herald Press, 1967.

Good, Merle and Phyllis. *Twenty Most Asked Questions About the Amish and Mennonites.* Intercourse, Pennsylvania: Good Books, 1979.

Good, Merle. *Who Are The Amish?* Intercourse, Pennsylvania: Good Books, 1985.

Hess, Willis A., and Hess, Ray B. *Minutes of the Annual Meetings of the Old German Baptist Brethren.* Winona Lake, Indiana: BMH Printing, 1981.

Hoover, Amos B. *The Jonas Martin Era.* n.p. Amos B. Hoover, 1982. Documentary sources on the Old Order Mennonite divisions.

Horst, Isaac R. *Separate and Peculiar.* Mt. Forest, Ontario: Isaac R. Horst, 1979. A description of the Old Order Mennonites of Ontario.

Hostetler, John A. *Amish Society.* Baltimore, Maryland: Johns Hopkins University Press, 1980.

Kraybill, Donald B. *The Riddle of Amish Culture.* Baltimore, Maryland: Johns Hopkins University Press, 1988. The "why" behind Amish practices.

The Mennonite Encyclopedia. Scottdale, Pennsylvania: Herald Press, 1959, 1972.

Ruth, John L. *A Quiet and Peaceable Life.* Intercourse, Pennsylvania: Good Books, 1979, 1985.

Scott, Stephen E. *Plain Buggies.* Intercourse, Pennsylvania: Good Books, 1981.

Scott, Stephen E. *Why Do They Dress That Way?* Intercourse, Pennsylvania: Good Books, 1986.

Seitz, Ruth and Blair. *Amish Country.* New York: Crescent, 1987.

Yoder, Joseph W. *Rosanna of the Amish.* Scottdale, Pennsylvania: Herald Press, 1969. Contains a detailed description of an Amish wedding.

Yoder, Joseph W. *Amische Lieder.* Huntingdon, Pennsylvania: Yoder Publishing Co., 1942. Amish hymns and songs with musical notation.

Articles

Beachy, Monroe. "Decided by Lot," *Family Life* (October 1969), 20–22.

Bryer, Kathleen B. "The Amish Way of Death," *American Psychologist,* Vol. 34, No. 3 (March 1979), 255–261.

Hostetler, Beulah S. "An Old Order River Brethren Love Feast," *Pennsylvania Folklife,* Vol. 24, (Winter 1974–75), 8–20.

Jackson, George Pullen. "Strange Music of the Old Order Amish," *Musical Quarterly,* XXXI No. 3 (July 1945), 275–288.

Jentsch, Theodore W. "Old Order Mennonite Life of East Penn Valley," *Pennsylvania Folklife,* XX No. 1 (1974), 18–27.

Luthy, David. "A Survey of Amish Ordination Customs," *Family Life* (March 1975), 13–17.

Luthy, David. "Replacing the Ausbund," *Family Life* (November 1981), 21–23.

Schlabach, David R. "En Amishchi Leicht" (An Amish Funeral), in *Cemetery Directory of the Amish Community in Eastern Holmes and Adjoining Counties in Ohio* by Leroy Beachy. n.p. Leroy Beachy, 1975.

Scott, Stephen E. "The Old Order River Brethren," *Pennsylvania Mennonite Heritage*, Vol. I, No. 3 (July 1978), 13–22.

Stayer, Jonathan R. "An Interpretation of Some Ritual and Food Elements of the Brethren Love Feast," *Pennsylvania Folklife*, Vol. 34, No. 2 (Winter 1984–85), 61–70.

Stull, Paul H. "Annual Meeting," *The Vindicator* (May 1977), 131–136.

Umble, John. "The Old Order Amish, Their Hymns and Hymn Tunes," *Journal of American Folklore*, Vol. III (1939), 82–95.

Umble, John. "Amish Service Manuals," *Mennonite Quarterly Review*, 15 (January 1941), 26–32.

Zimmerman, Elsie. "Old Order Mennonite Weddings," *Historic Sheafferstown Record*, Vol. 21, No. 2 (April 1987).

Dissertations

Cronk, Sandra. *Gelassenheit: The Rites of the Redemptive Process in Old Order Amish and Old Order Mennonite Communities*. Ph.D. Dissertation, University of Chicago, 1977.

Huntington, Gertrude Enders. *Dove at the Window: A Study of an Old Order Amish Community in Ohio*. Ph.D. Dissertation, Yale University, 1957.

Jentsch, Theodore W. *Mennonite Americans: A Study of a Religious Subculture from a Sociological Perspective*. Ph.D. Dissertation, University of South Africa, 1973. A study of the Wenger Mennonites.

Periodicals

Die Botschaft. Brookshire Publications, Lancaster, Pennsylvania. A weekly newsletter for Old Order groups.

The Budget. Budget Publishing Company, Sugarcreek, Ohio. A weekly paper featuring news from hundreds of plain communities.

Calvary Messenger. Calvary Publications, Meyersdale, Pennsylvania. The monthly magazine of the Beachy Amish.

Christian Contender. Rod and Staff Publishers, Crockett, Kentucky. A monthly magazine published by conservative Mennonites.

The Diary. Pequea Publishers, Gordonville, Pennsylvania. A monthly Old Order Amish news magazine.

Family Life. Pathway Publishing House, Aylmer, Ontario. An Old Order Amish monthly magazine.

The Vindicator. Union City, Ohio. The monthly periodical of the Old German Baptist Brethren.

Hymnals

Ausbund, 1564. Primary hymnal for most Old Order Amish.

Eine Unpartheyisches Gesangbuch, 1804. Primary hymnal of Old Order Mennonites in Pennsylvania and youth hymnal for Lancaster and Nebraska Amish.

Die Gemeinschaftliche Lieder-Sammlung, 1836. Primary hymnal of Ontario and Indiana Old Order Mennonites.

Eine Unparteiische Lieder-Sammlung (Baer Book), 1860. Primary hymnal of Old Order Amish in Somerset County, Pennsylvania; Kalona, Iowa; and Arthur, Illinois. Youth hymnal in most Amish communities.

Unparteiische Liedersammlung (Guengerich Book), 1892. Primary hymnal of Old Order Amish in Daviess County, Indiana.

Mennonite Hymns, 1847. Primary hymnal of Horning, Markham and Wisler Mennonites.

Mennonite Hymnal, 1928. Primary hymnal of Old Order Mennonites in Virginia.

A Collection of Hymns, Songs and Sacred Songs, 1882. Primary hymnal of Old German Baptist Brethren and related groups.

Spiritual Hymns, 1874 and 1980. Primary hymnals of Old Order River Brethren.

Index

About the Author

Stephen Scott grew up in southwestern Ohio near a large community of Old German Baptist Brethren. In his youth, he became impressed with the life of the plain people. He visited various plain groups in Ohio and eventually worked, lived and worshipped with them.

In 1969 Steve moved to Lancaster County, Pennsylvania. He is now a member of the Old Order River Brethren, one of the plain groups described in this book.

Steve studied at Cedarville (Ohio) College and has been a teacher. He is the author of *Plain Buggies: Amish, Mennonite, and Brethren Horse-Drawn Transportation* and *Why Do They Dress That Way?*, a book about plain clothing. In addition, he helped collect data and made maps and historical charts for the Holmes County, Ohio, and Geauga County, Ohio, Amish directories. He researched, drew and published the map *The Plain Churches and Related Groups of Lancaster County, Pennsylvania* and has written articles for *The Brethren Encyclopedia, Pennsylvania Mennonite Heritage* and *The Diary*.

Steve married Harriet Sauder in 1973. The Scotts have three children and live near Columbia, Pennsylvania. Steve works as a researcher for Good Enterprises of Intercourse, Pennsylvania.